REVISED AND EXPANDED

Women Reaching Women

IN CRISIS
MINISTRY HANDBOOK

COMPILED by
CHRIS ADAMS

© 2005 LifeWay Press®
Revised and expanded 2014

All assessment tests offered in this book may be photocopied and reproduced for participants. No other part of this book may be reproduced or transmitted in any form or by any means, electronic or mechanical, including photocopying and recording, or by any information storage or retrieval system, except as may be expressly permitted in writing by the publisher. Requests for permission should be addressed in writing to LifeWay Press®; One LifeWay Plaza; Nashville, TN 37234-0152.

Dewey decimal classification: 259
Subject headings: WOMEN \ MINISTRY \ CHURCH WORK WITH WOMEN

Item 005693366
ISBN 978-1-4300-3653-1

Unless otherwise noted, all Scripture quotations are taken from Holman Christian Standard Bible®, copyright © 1999, 2000, 2002, 2003 by Holman Bible Publishers.

Scripture quotations marked (The Message) are taken from The Message. Copyright © 1993, 1994, 1995, 1996, 2000, 2001, 2002. Used by permission of NavPress Publishing Group.

Scripture quotations identified NIV are from the Holy Bible, New International Version, copyright © 1973, 1978, 1984 by International Bible Society. Used by permission.

Scripture quotations marked (NLT) are taken from the Holy Bible, New Living Translation, copyright ©1996. Used by permission of Tyndale House Publishers, Inc., Wheaton, IL 60189 USA. All rights reserved.

To order additional copies of this resource, write to LifeWay Church Resources Customer Service; One LifeWay Plaza; Nashville, TN 37234-0113; fax 615.251.5933; phone 800.458.2772; email orderentry@lifeway.com; order online at www.lifeway.com; or visit the LifeWay Christian Store serving you.

Printed in the United States of America

Adult Ministry Publishing
LifeWay Christian Resources
One LifeWay Plaza
Nashville, TN 37234-0152

CONTENTS

INTRODUCTION

Jacque Truitt, Barney Self, and Chris Adams

As a leader of women in your church, have you ever had a woman call you, stop you in the hall, or come into your office and begin sharing a crisis that you felt totally unable to handle? Perhaps she told you about the abuse she is experiencing in her marriage, the abortions she has had, the sexual molestation forced upon her as a child, or the recent tragic death of a child. Often we do not do anything because we just do not know what to do.

Have you personally experienced any of the previous issues or perhaps another, such as infertility, a prodigal child, or a painful divorce? What did you do as you found restoration, peace, and healing? Did you ever think God might be able to use your experience in the life of another woman?

God wants to use women to help other women dealing with crisis. He also desires to redeem our own experiences to walk in understanding with other women dealing with experiences similar to ours. *Women Reaching Women in Crisis* was developed to assist you as a leader to know how to help women in pain or how to refer them to others if you don't have the ability to help.

The specific crisis issues in this series are
1. substance abuse
2. post-abortion trauma
3. domestic violence and spouse abuse
4. depression
5. prodigal children
6. sexual addiction
7. infertility

Our hope is that you will find this series helpful as you minister to women in your church and others your ministry touches. We also hope you will use this series to encourage others in your women's ministry to be leaders. **(Note: You have permission to photocopy and distribute all assessment tests in this book.)**

From 1 Timothy 3:1-13, we learn qualifications of church leaders.

> This saying is trustworthy: "If anyone aspires to be an overseer, he desires a noble work." An overseer, therefore, must be above reproach, the husband of one wife, self-controlled, sensible, respectable, hospitable, an able teacher, not addicted to wine, not a bully but gentle, not quarrelsome, not greedy—one who manages his own household competently, having his children under control with all dignity. (If anyone does not know how to manage his own household, how will he take care of God's church?) He must not be a new convert, or he might become conceited and fall into the condemnation of the Devil. Furthermore, he must have a good reputation among outsiders, so that he does not fall into disgrace and the Devil's trap.

> Deacons, likewise, should be worthy of respect, not hypocritical, not drinking a lot of wine, not greedy for money, holding the mystery of the faith with a clear conscience. And they must also be tested first; if they prove blameless, then they can serve as deacons. Wives, too, must be worthy of respect, not slanderers, self-controlled, faithful in everything. Deacons must be husbands of one wife, managing their children and their own households competently. For those who have served well as deacons acquire a good standing for themselves, and great boldness in the faith that is in Christ Jesus.

Here's a compiled list of qualifications:
- above reproach
- the husband of one wife
- self-controlled
- sensible
- respectable
- hospitable
- an able teacher
- not addicted to wine/not drinking a lot of wine
- not a bully but gentle
- not quarrelsome
- not greedy (for money)
- one who manages his own household competently
- having his children under control with all dignity
- not be a new convert
- have a good reputation among outsiders
- should be worthy of respect
- not hypocritical
- holding the mystery of the faith with a clear conscience
- not slanderers
- faithful in everything

Don't panic! Not every one of us has all of these qualifications. As we mature in Christ, these characteristics develop more like Him. Let's look at how some of those qualifications relate to our role as a helper for women in crisis.

- **Spiritual maturity.** A woman in a helping role should have a good knowledge of Scripture and demonstrate wisdom in applying it to her life. She should demonstrate a regular prayer life. She should not be a new believer.

- **Psychological and emotional stability.** A Christian leader should be psychologically and emotionally stable. She should be open and vulnerable. This doesn't mean that she should be perfect and "have it all together." But, a woman in leadership needs to be able to control her emotions and not be prone to outbursts. She needs to have a healthy sense of who she is as a woman in Christ.

- **Moral lifestyle.** She should be known as a godly woman. In addition to the qualifications found in 1 Timothy 3, examine Proverbs 31:10-31.

> Who can find a capable wife?
>> She is far more precious than jewels.
> The heart of her husband trusts in her,
>> and he will not lack anything good.
> She rewards him with good, not evil, all the days of her life.
> She selects wool and flax and works with willing hands.
> She is like the merchant ships, bringing her food from far away.

She rises while it is still night and provides food
    for her household and portions for her servants.
She evaluates a field and buys it;
    she plants a vineyard with her earnings.
She draws on her strength and reveals that her arms are strong.
She sees that her profits are good,
    and her lamp never goes out at night.
She extends her hands to the spinning staff,
    and her hands hold the spindle.
Her hands reach out to the poor,
    and she extends her hands to the needy.
She is not afraid for her household when it snows,
    for all in her household are doubly clothed.
She makes her own bed coverings;
    her clothing is fine linen and purple.
Her husband is known at the city gates,
    where he sits among the elders of the land.
She makes and sells linen garments;
    she delivers belts to the merchants.
Strength and honor are her clothing,
    and she can laugh at the time to come.
She opens her mouth with wisdom,
    and loving instruction is on her tongue.
She watches over the activities of her household
    and is never idle.
Her sons rise up and call her blessed.
    Her husband also praises her:
"Many women are capable, but you surpass them all!"
Charm is deceptive and beauty is fleeting,
    but a woman who fears the LORD will be praised.
Give her the reward of her labor,
    and let her works praise her at the city gates.

- **Spiritual gifts.** Leaders should demonstrate the presence of spiritual gifts appropriate to ministry (such as mercy, exhortation, teaching, discernment).

- **Care and interest in people.** A Christian leader will demonstrate a warm, caring, and genuine interest in people and their well-being.

- **Availability.** A woman in ministry needs to have the time to be trained, supervised, and involved in ministry. Being available doesn't mean that you lose your personal life. After all, you need time to refresh and grow personally as you mature in Christ.

- **Teachability.** A leader needs to have a teachable spirit and attitude. She should be willing to learn and grow in the training process.

- **Ability to maintain healthy boundaries.** The very essence of good ministry is to inspire these women to be self-reliant and determined. They should not be dependent on others in an unhealthy way.

- **Life experience.** The leader should have some life experiences; that is, she should not be too young to have gained some life-learned insights. However, you can't experience everything! In the cases where you don't have personal experience, ask the Lord to help you express a personal connection to the women to whom you're listening and ministering. You can also seek counsel from other leaders.

- **Confidentiality.** The leader should always maintain confidentiality and protect the privacy of those who come to her for help.

What are some basic skills necessary to listen to women in crisis? We will examine several to help us minister to our best ability.

Avoid Common Communication Barriers

Certain verbal phrases and nonverbal approaches tend to shut down communication. As lay ministers, we want to avoid these common pitfalls. Consider the following tactics and statements that become barriers to communication:

- Advising, giving solutions.
  "Why don't you just tell your husband to spend more time with you?"
- Directing, commanding.
  "Stop talking such nonsense; you'll be all right."
  "You get that notion out of your head right now."
- Moralizing, preaching.
  "You ought to look at the bright side."
  "You should pray more about it.
- Disagreeing, blaming.
  "You're not thinking clearly, if that's how you feel."
  "You're off base to think everyone has deserted you."
- Ridiculing, shaming, and labeling.
  "You're acting very immature."
  "How can you say that when so many are worse off than you?"
- Praising, agreeing.
  "I agree that people have mistreated you."
  "Well, you're just more perceptive than she is."
- Warning, promising.
  "If you will calm down, I'll listen to you."
  "If you stay in that mood, you will just get worse."
- Giving logical argument, lecturing.
  "Why don't you …?"
- Probing, questioning, interrogating.
  "Why did you do that?"

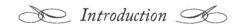

- Withdrawing, humor, sarcasm, diversion.
- Reassuring, sympathizing, consoling.
  "You poor thing."
- Interpreting, analyzing, diagnosing.
  "You did that because … ?"
  "I think that dream means …"

Remember the Importance of Confidentiality

Consider it a privilege when someone turns to you for help. You have received the gift of trust. Do not betray that trust or trivialize it by gossiping about others' misfortune. Always ask permission before sharing someone's privileged information with family members, prayer partners, church staff, or anyone else.

Hold your tongue; respect yourself as well as the person who confided in you. The only exception to confidentiality is the rule of safety. If someone shares that they plan to harm herself or someone else, you are legally responsible to help keep them safe even if it means betraying their trust.

Recognize Your Own Vulnerability

As you minister to someone who hurts, you hurt. When she mourns, you mourn. Don't deny your personal feelings. Feed yourself emotionally and spiritually so you can continue to care for and nurture others.

Evaluate Your Motives for Becoming Involved

- Do you see yourself as a rescuer trying to save your victim?
- What are your expectations of the person you're helping?
- Do you expect gratefulness?
- Do you put a price tag on your caring?

In reality, the hurting person may feel embarrassed or ashamed by admitting weakness. If she feels she's failed you (although untrue), she may gradually pull away from you, creating an awkward distance. Often in our ministry and love for someone, we may be called to let go to allow her to grow, to develop, and to reach beyond our own limiting vision. Keep your vulnerability in check as you seek to minister.

Know Your Limitations

Lay ministry is not counseling or therapy. Recognize when to refer someone to a professional counselor or therapist. Often listening and caring are not sufficient help. Some tasks fall outside the scope of lay ministry. A lay minister would not attempt to set a broken leg if she were not a doctor. Likewise, she should not attempt to provide the intense help required for circumstances such as rape or abuse.

Lay people sometimes hesitate to minister because they think they are expected to counsel. Therefore, hurting individuals often fail to receive the help and encouragement they need. An effective lay minister understands how to support and encourage hurting women without feeling compelled to solve their problems.

Referrals

When a woman comes to you or another leader with her struggles, you may find yourself maxed out in terms of knowledge, experience, time, or personal involvement. At that point, it's time to seek other ways within your church or community to help this individual (and her husband/family when appropriate).

Here are 10 scenarios that merit referral to a professional Christian counselor.

1. The amount of time necessary to help her exceeds your time as a caregiver. Taking care of others in these situations must not take over your life. Balance is essential.

2. Her struggles are beyond your emotional resources. When working with others in a caregiving role, you must monitor your emotional state to make certain that the process is not damaging emotional viability.

3. You don't have the physical energy to help the individual. You can easily develop fatigue while caregiving, and continuing to give in a depleted state can be dangerous to you and the woman involved.

4. You don't have the expertise to help this individual. Often, a hurting woman's issues may be greater than your ability to provide help. Others who are more thoroughly trained can provide greater care that will move the individual toward healing. Ask yourself, "Is my care the best care possible?"

5. Continuing to provide care could be harmful to the individual, you, or your family. Caregiving can unintentionally promote dependence by the counselee on the caregiver, which is called *enabling* and can cause harm to all involved.

6. You have a "dual relationship" with the woman you are trying to help. A dual relationship is a situation where you wear more than one hat in the life of the counselee. For example, are you a cell group leader, an accountability partner, or a ministry leader trying to assist a woman in your group? The dual relationship may cause confusion as to which hat you're wearing. This dual relationship can be worked through, but it can be risky.

7. Despite your efforts, it appears the individual is getting worse. It does not matter how well-intentioned she may be—if your attempt to assist is not working, then referral to another caregiver is a healthy option when all other avenues have been exhausted.

8. The woman becomes a threat to herself or to others. When an individual threatens suicide, it must always be taken seriously. Referral or intensive connection or both may be necessary to deal with the crisis this creates.

When someone is suicidal, do whatever is necessary to keep them safe from themselves. If it means calling in her family to watch until she can be hospitalized, going to sit with her in the emergency room, clearing out the medicine cabinet, or removing a gun from the premises, do it. If the woman gets upset or threatens you, recognize that you may be the only lifeline she has at that moment. To distance or disconnect at that moment might mean the end of her life. This is not the time to be kind. It is the time to be lovingly expeditious. Involving authorities is helpful because it can remove you from the power spot. Knowing someone's counselor's or physician's phone number can be critical in those times, again to put someone else in that position of ultimate responsibility. However, when there is no one else, you may be that responsible party.

9. Personality differences can limit your ability to make a positive difference in her life. Sometimes there is just not a fit with someone who needs help. That disparity must be accounted for, and referral may be the best alternative for making certain she gets the assistance she needs.

10. The spiritual issues involved are beyond your understanding. If spiritual issues are beyond your ability to provide support or understanding, it may be appropriate to refer her to your pastor or another leader who can better assist in the spiritual struggle and theological understanding. Talk to her about this option to be sure she is open to this potential change.

You don't have to bear the burden of lay counseling alone. It's important to know when to draw your boundaries in caregiving and bring in professional help. By generally assessing the well-being of the individual, your involvement as a lay counselor, and the health of the lay counseling situation, you can be better equipped to help a woman in crisis get back on track.

Warning Signs

Assessment of the individual's needs on an ongoing basis is very important. The following are elements that need to be assessed and that might suggest that a referral is warranted.

Behavioral Signs
- Sudden changes in social behavior (becoming unusually outgoing or withdrawn)
- Inability to concentrate
- Lethargy or listlessness
- Power struggles with authority

- Hyperactivity or nervousness
- Loss of interest in favorite activities
- A major change in friendship groups
- Inability to make decisions
- Confusion about career goals

Emotional Signs

- Open talk about intense family problems
- Marital distress resulting in emotional or physical trauma
- Overwhelming sadness following the death or serious illness of a family member or friend
- Feeling blue, sad, unhappy, or down in the dumps
- Mood swings
- Fluctuation between silence and talkativeness
- Pessimism, hopelessness, or helplessness about the future
- Preoccupation with physical/sexual issues
- Extreme suspiciousness or irrational feeling of persecution
- Nonsensical conversation, indications of being out of touch with reality
- Persistent lying, stealing, or other antisocial behaviors
- Marked lack of response to normally upsetting events
- Erratic behavior
- Crying spells
- Recurring thoughts of suicide or death
- Unwarranted sense of tremendous guilt
- Feeling inadequate or like a failure

Physical Signs

- A marked change in weight or appearance
- Excessive eating
- Extreme loss of appetite or excessive preoccupation with weight issues
- A marked change in sleeping habits
- Poor hygiene
- Becoming more accident prone
- Frequent illness
- Feeling consistently tired and fatigued
- Use of alcohol or drugs to cope with life's traumas
- Problems with concentration, memory, or attention
- Angry outbursts

We are made in three parts as Scripture defines us: body, mind, and spirit. When life gets chaotic, encourage the women who come to you to account for their well-being in that order. Physical issues need to be addressed with their primary care physician. It's vital for individuals to establish such a relationship if they do not already have one.

Emotionally, it is good to work with a competent therapist who will approach the individual from a biblical perspective. Finally, it is critical that the individual have a healthy relationship with the pastor or pastoral caregiver. The theological issues at play and God's care in their midst need to be a central focus in the recovery process. When an individual struggles, it is essential that she get the very best help to experience the abundant life God desperately wants for her.

Networking

Every minister needs to have a network of competent Christian professionals who can serve as referral sources. The most obvious place to begin the quest for those resources is in the local church.

- Determine who are the competent doctors, therapists, or counselors in your church. Many churches have lists they have compiled over a number of years. Physicians and therapists in your church can also be used as resources for finding other professionals who are both competent in their specialty and focused on a vital and personal relationship with God.

- Use other churches' lists of referrals. Churches in the local area that are healthy, evangelistic, and biblically based will likely have a list of care providers. One option is to call a church you trust and ask, "I am a minister at XYZ Church and was wondering if you had a list of counselors you trust. One of my church members is in need of help. Would you mind sharing those names with me, please?" Before adding these recommended names to your list of trusted caregivers, do some research on each person. Questions to ask are found later in this chapter.

- Use the phone book. Often Christians will note their advertisement with an *ichthus,* or fish-type symbol. Some communities have a directory of Christian organizations and individuals. Research these individuals as you would others you don't know personally.

- Use Christian organizations. In metropolitan areas, groups of physicians and therapists may form organizations like Christian Medical Fellowship or Christian Counselors Fellowship. These groups may provide invaluable assistance in networking with godly caregivers.

- Connect with the local denominational association. The local Baptist association is a potential resource for information, networking, and referral. Often directors of missions have been in a given area for extended periods of time and know a number of the caregivers personally.

- Use Southern Baptist state minister relations personnel. Most states have a person designated as a caregiver for the ministry body. Many of these persons have developed trusted lists of caregivers in each area of their state(s) and may be willing to share that information upon request.

- Seek information from various national organizations.
The American Association of Christian Counselors: *www.aacc.net*
The American Association of Pastoral Counselors: *www.aapc.org*
Focus on the Family: *www.family.org*. The pastoral care line is (877) 233-4455 and is available Monday through Friday, 6 a.m. to 8 p.m., MT. Focus on the Family Counseling line is (855) 771-HELP and is available Monday through Friday, 6 a.m. to 8 p.m., MT.
Celebrate Recovery: *www.celebraterecovery.co*m

- Question the trust level for referrals whenever lists are used from sources other than personal recommendation. That doesn't mean these people shouldn't be trusted; it means that trust is an earned commodity.

  Ask two questions to gauge caregivers and their ability to be trusted:

  1. *Is the problem (depression, prodigal child, sexual abuse or addiction, substance abuse, or domestic violence and spousal abuse) within your scope of practice?* A therapist has an ethical responsibility to inform you honestly if the presenting problem is or is not within his or her training and experience.

  2. *How do you integrate psychology and theology in your practice?* What you want to hear—without asking for it directly—is that the professional counselor uses scriptural reference points in therapy and that they are willing to pray with the client in the process of therapy.

- Determine if other groups in your area are striving to provide similar resources for those in need. Connecting with others committed to assisting those in need and utilizing their understanding can create a win-win scenario of shared information.

About the Authors

JACQUE TRUITT is a licensed marriage and family therapist and co-author of *Shelter from the Storm: Hope for Survivors of Sexual Abuse* (and author of the facilitators guide for that text). Her articles on marriage and family issues, substance abuse, sexual abuse, and women's issues have been published in national magazines.

BARNEY SELF, EdD, is a licensed marriage and family therapist who has practiced for the past 30 years in Nashville and works as Pastoral Counseling Minister on staff with Forest Hills Baptist Church in Nashville, Tennessee.

CHRIS ADAMS is the senior lead specialist in women's ministry training and events of LifeWay Christian Resources of the Southern Baptist Convention. She has compiled *Women Reaching Women: Beginning and Building a Women's Enrichment Ministry* and *Transformed Lives: Taking Women's Ministry to the Next Level.*

 NOTES

1

SUBSTANCE ABUSE

Karla Downing

This chapter seeks to provide information for those who minister to persons experiencing substance abuse. Through this chapter you will become familiar with characteristics, behaviors, and terms associated with substance abuse. You'll also read some of what God has to say about abusing substances. Finally, you will be provided with practical tools to enable you to help other women. As you seek to help, your purpose is to inform, support, encourage, and refer the woman who has placed her trust in you.

God's View

Ask several Christians their views of drinking alcohol and you'll get a myriad of answers. Some people hold to strict abstention, believing it is wrong for a Christian to drink any alcohol. Others feel comfortable drinking small amounts such as wine with meals or an occasional beer or mixed drink.

The Bible clearly tells us not to be drunk and to remain alert and in control of our actions at all times, but it does not necessarily tell us we cannot drink.

> Don't get drunk with wine, which leads to reckless actions.
> Ephesians 5:18
>
> Be sober! Be on the alert! Your adversary the Devil is prowling around like a roaring lion, looking for anyone he can devour.
> 1 Peter 5:8

Romans 14 says that each of us has to live according to our own consciences in "doubtful issues" such as food, drink, and which days are observed for the Lord (v. 1). However, we must keep in mind that when our actions cause a weaker Christian brother (or sister) to stumble, we should abstain because we do not want to "tear down God's work because of food. Everything is clean, but it is wrong for a man to cause stumbling by what he eats. It is a noble thing not to eat meat, or drink wine, or do anything that makes your brother (or sister) stumble" (Romans 14:20-21).

The final test for believers is that anything that hinders our Christian walk needs to be put aside.

> Since we also have such a large cloud of witnesses surrounding us, let us lay aside every weight and the sin that so easily ensnares us, and run with endurance the race that lies before us.
> Hebrews 12:1

Authors mention wine several times in the New Testament. Jesus' first miracle was at a wedding where He turned water into wine. You can find this story in John 2:1-11.

Paul instructed Timothy to drink wine to help his physical problems.

> Don't continue drinking only water, but use a little wine because of your stomach and your frequent illnesses.
> 1 Timothy 5:23

Paul warned overseers and deacons to do everything in moderation and "not [be] addicted to wine … not drinking a lot of wine" (1 Timothy 3:3,8).

The Greek word for drugs is *pharmakia,* which refers to the use of drugs, potions, and spells by someone involved in sorcery or witchcraft. Galatians 5:20-21 lists both sorcery and drunkenness as a work of the flesh.

The use of drugs in moderation for emotional illness, pain relief, or management of medical problems is not wrong. However, Scripture does not support being addicted to drugs or using mind-altering drugs that harm the body and result in wrong actions while under the influence.

As a ministry leader, you will eventually encounter women who are dealing with substance abuse. Either they or their husbands are dependent on a substance. Or it might be that their children or other family members are using and the abuse is directly affecting this woman.

Let's get acquainted with some terms you might hear as you seek to help those who are experiencing substance abuse.

Abuse and Dependence

Throughout this chapter you will see the word "addict" used to describe a man or woman whose life is controlled by drugs, alcohol, or any other substance or behavior. You will also see the word "alcoholic" used to refer specifically to someone addicted to alcohol.

Substance abuse and dependence involve the overuse of alcohol, prescription drugs, and illegal drugs. People often start out using drugs and alcohol socially, to relax, or to cope with stress and emotional pain. Prescription drugs are often taken initially to relieve pain or deal with anxiety or depression. Eventually, some people come to rely on the drug and become addicted.

According to the *Diagnostic and Statistical Manual of Mental Disorders* (fourth edition, text revision, DSM-IV-TR, American Psychiatric Association, Washington, DC, 2000), a difference exists between substance abuse and substance dependence.

"Abuse" occurs when people experience adverse effects in one or more areas of life: legal, social, or occupational. They may find themselves missing work or getting in more conflicts as a result of using. They may even use the substance in risky situations such as driving a car or operating machinery.

"Dependence" occurs when the person cannot stop using the substance, takes larger quantities than desired, continues to use despite known adverse effects such as a threat to their health, and experiences tolerance or withdrawal. In addition, more time is spent on obtaining the substance, using it, and recovering from the effects. Dependence is also referred to as addiction.

Varying substances have different abilities to cause addiction. Some result in addiction almost from the first time they are taken; others may take a substantial amount of time. Some cause psychological and physiological addiction and some only psychological. Some addicts use multiple substances to moderate the effects of each one.

Substance abuse and addiction are present in all socioeconomic spheres and occupations. Some people seem to be more susceptible than others to becoming addicted. Many believe some people have an addictive personality that is compulsive and obsessive and easily hooked into not only substances but also other addictions such as gambling, sexual addiction, cigarette smoking, and work. Others disagree that an addictive personality exists and say the addictive process itself results in the compulsions and obsessions. The question revolves around whether the addict's obsession comes before or after the addiction.

Some addicts will go through the stages quicker than others, but generally addiction follows a predictable progression. In the beginning, no obvious problems are evident. The user enjoys the use of the substance and may even perform better while using. Later, craving, which is a strong desire for the substance that is not relieved until the substance is taken, begins. At some point, the user begins to depend on the substance and expect it at certain times and events, feeling agitated or uncomfortable when not able to use. Tolerance occurs as the person uses the substance repeatedly. Tolerance has to do with needing an increased amount of a substance to get the same effect or the decreased effectiveness of the substance at the usual amount that occurs as the result of repeated use. In other words, they have to take more of it. Tolerance is the first sign of addiction.

In the late stage, addicts lose control over the substance and spend most of their energy on using and trying not to use. They experience increasing difficulties in multiple areas of their lives. Their health deteriorates. They may lose jobs, devastate their finances, and get into legal trouble.

Psychological difficulties increase: instability, loss of emotional control, low self-esteem, difficulty concentrating, and memory loss. Emotions increase in intensity: anger, depression, anxiety, and agitation.

Addicts in the later stages experience blackouts. A blackout is a period when the person under the influence of drugs or alcohol appears to be functioning normally but doesn't remember anything. It can be dangerous, as addicts will do and say things they later regret. Some have entered into bad business deals and other commitments. Some have conflicts and altercations with family members and friends they later do not remember. Others wake up in strange places and wonder how they got there.

The ability to control the use of a substance temporarily does not prove a person is not an addict, although addicts will say it does. As long as addicts can point to a time they don't use, they think they're not addicted. This is one way that the addict maintains the denial of the addiction. Most addicts can abstain for a short time, especially before the later stages of the disease. The problem is maintaining abstinence, which is something they cannot do. The truth is that non-addicts don't have any need to control their use of a substance; only addicts do. Family members often recognize addiction earlier than the addict.

The Personality of the Addict

Alcoholics Anonymous calls addictive thinking "stinkin' thinkin'" to describe the difficult personality characteristics that addicts often exhibit whether or not they are under the influence. When the addict is not under the influence, this behavior is referred to as the "dry drunk syndrome." A "dry drunk" is someone who experiences without being intoxicated the same irrational thought processes and moods the addict experiences when under the influence.

Addicts often display grandiosity. This is when the addict has an exaggerated sense of his or her own importance, abilities, knowledge, accomplishments, or significance. Or the opposite might be true—feeling an exaggerated sense of self-pity. In this state, the addict will be demanding and intolerant of others, unable to delay gratification, judgmental, indecisive, and impulsive.

Mood swings are common and the addict may exhibit a dark and somber mood with a tendency to withdraw from others. He or she may appear nostalgic and overly emotional or sentimental. The addict may fantasize about escaping through the use of the substance or by a change in outward circumstances such as changing jobs or locations. An addict's predominant attitude is often being arrogant, self-righteous, self-absorbed, and self-centered.

Over-reactions are typical. An over-reaction is a reaction that is not related to the actual seriousness or significance of the event or a reaction that normally would not trigger a similar response. The addict is unable to be introspective to gain understanding how his or her thinking and emotions are affecting the current situation, resulting in an inability to accept personal responsibility for the mood or reaction. This frequently results in blaming others.

Addicts display emotionally immature behavior. Generally, emotional growth stops when the addict begins using the substance. Addicts are often volatile and difficult to predict. Quite often, it's impossible to please them. If he or she asks for an egg sunny-side up, you'll be told that you left the wrong side up! The result is that the family begins to "walk on eggshells," carefully monitoring their actions, responses, emotions, and words, so they don't upset the addict and set off an emotional deluge.

Addicts have a distorted low self-image. Many have difficulty with establishing relationships. The use of drugs or alcohol masks feelings of inferiority. Under the influence, they have a false sense of confidence. While they may use to cover their low self-esteem, when they see the carnage from their using, they feel worse about themselves. Guilt is typically experienced as shame. Shame tells them that they are unworthy and bad, rather than their behavior being bad. The shame is overwhelming and often drives them back to using. The original source of shame is often abuse, neglect, and dysfunctional family dynamics experienced as children.

God doesn't want us to experience shame. He loves and values each of us and sees us as worthy of redemption and restoration. He wants us to admit what we do wrong and change directions, but shame tends to do the opposite. Shame keeps us stuck in bad behavior because in our core being, we do not see ourselves as capable or worthy of change.

Christians struggling with substance abuse experience the shame of admitting that even with God's strength, they are powerless over this addiction. In the church, drinking and using drugs are often viewed as sin and character weakness. This attitude toward the addict can hinder his or her willingness to get help. Understanding the dynamics of addiction will help you to see that the addict is dealing with a condition that is more complex than simple willpower alone can conquer.

Let's examine alcoholism and drug abuse separately. Although they have similar characteristics, some differences exist.

Alcoholism

Proverbs 23:29-35 describes an alcoholic's anguish as follows:
> Who has woe? Who has sorrow?
> Who has conflicts? Who has complaints?
> Who has wounds for no reason?
> Who has red eyes?
> Those who linger over wine,
> those who go looking for mixed wine.
> Don't gaze at wine when it is red,
> when it gleams in the cup
> and goes down smoothly.
> In the end it bites like a snake
> and stings like a viper.
> Your eyes will see strange things,
> and you will say absurd things.
> You'll be like someone sleeping out at sea
> or lying down on the top of a ship's mast.
> "They struck me, but I feel no pain!
> They beat me, but I didn't know it!
> When will I wake up?
> I'll look for another drink."

A Drinker or an Alcoholic?

Generally an alcoholic is someone whose drinking negatively, regularly, and increasingly affects any aspect of life: physical, mental, emotional, social, relational, or spiritual.

Alcoholics Anonymous states the following: "If, when you honestly want to, you find you cannot quit entirely, or if when drinking, you have little control over the amount you take, you are probably an alcoholic," (*Alcoholics Anonymous,* Third Edition, Alcoholics Anonymous World Services, Inc., New York City, 1976, p. 44). Some of the people who have a few drinks at night to relax are actually in the initial stages of alcoholism. They may or may not progress to later stages of addiction.

Some alcoholics are periodic drinkers. They can go for long periods of time without drinking, but when they drink, they cannot stop and find themselves going on binges that last days or weeks. Regardless of the drinking pattern, the factor that distinguishes a drinker from an alcoholic is whether he or she can stop once starting.

Evidence points to a genetic factor in alcoholism, although the specific factor is unknown. More children of alcoholics become alcoholics than the children of non-alcoholics. Alcoholics metabolize alcohol differently than non-alcoholics. Some alcoholics state that from the very first drink, they were hooked. Others report that they felt normal for the first time after taking a drink.

Alcohol is a depressant or tranquilizer, but it initially appears to have a stimulating effect by lowering inhibitions. Because of this, it can cause emotional instability and a depressed mood even when the effects have worn off. Many alcoholics function at their peak when they are drinking.

Women metabolize alcohol differently than men, so they will have a higher blood alcohol level after drinking the same amount of alcohol. Alcohol also tends to affect their emotions more. In addition, they have an increased susceptibility to alcohol related liver, heart, and brain damage.

Cessation of alcohol results in withdrawal symptoms. A hangover is a really mild withdrawal symptom, which is why drinking more alcohol gets rid of the hangover. Mild withdrawal symptoms include shakiness, insomnia, headache, eye ache, nausea, vomiting, increased perspiration, moodiness, and depression. More severe symptoms additionally include hand tremors, convulsions (severe shaking), anxiety, seizures, and in some cases delirium tremens (DTs). DTs involve seeing, hearing, or feeling things that are not real such as bugs or snakes crawling on the body. Withdrawal from prolonged and heavy use of alcohol can be life threatening.

Alcoholism is a terminal disease. If the drinker continues to drink, he or she will die from the effects on the body or from an accident. Alcohol is also related to neurological changes and can result in insanity or dementia.

Drugs

Drug addiction is a chronic, progressive, and potentially fatal disease. With repeated use, it causes psychological and physical damage and for some death.

Narcotics Anonymous describes addicts this way: "Our whole life and thinking was centered in drugs in one form or another—the getting and using and finding ways and means to get more. We lived to use and used to live. Very simply, an addict is a man or woman whose life is controlled by drugs. We are people in the grip of a continuing and progressive illness whose ends are always the same: jails, institutions and death," (*Narcotics Anonymous*, Fifth Ed., Narcotics Anonymous World Service Office, Inc., Van Nuys, CA, 1988, p. 3).

Many drugs are illegal to use, and sometimes drug addicts end up serving prison sentences for this crime. However, some states have laws like the one recently passed in California where drug offenders can be sent to rehabilitation instead of prison. Drugs can be expensive and require large quantities. Many users end up selling drugs or stealing, borrowing, or getting into debt to pay for their own, resulting in financial ruin or legal difficulties. Some even resort to prostitution.

A drug is "a substance that alters the physiology of the body but is not a food or nutrient," (*Drugs and Behavior: An Introduction to Behavioral Pharmacology*, Fifth Edition, William A. McKim, Prentice Hall, Upper Saddle River, New Jersey, 2003, p. 1). Drugs change body and brain chemistry. In order for the body to feel normal, it physically needs the drug. Tolerance develops because the body adapts to the drug and requires more of it to get the same effect. The psychological addiction occurs when the person depends on the drug to feel good or cope with life.

Drugs are ingested different ways: inhaled or smoked through the mouth or nose, injected intravenously, snorted through the nose, or swallowed orally in pill or liquid form. Drugs have short-term and long-term effects. Short-term effects result immediately from the current use and are part of the "high." Long-term effects result from the cumulative abuse of the drug on the body and mind. Many drugs can be lethal even if used only one time.

Drugs include both illegal street drugs and prescription drugs. Illegal drugs are sold on the black market by drug dealers and include substances like heroin, crack, cocaine, crystal methamphetamine, and marijuana.

Some drugs are obtainable both by prescription and through illegal means. Prescription drugs are often initially prescribed by doctors to control pain. People can become addicted, and when the doctor is no longer willing to give them the drug or they need larger quantities than the doctor is willing to prescribe, they continue to get the drug by illegal means, such as forging prescriptions, stealing from other people's medicine cabinets, buying it on the black market or the Internet, going to multiple doctors at a time for multiple prescriptions (referred to as doctor shopping), or having people fill prescriptions for them.

Prescription drug abuse is increasing with the easy availability of drugs on the Internet. One study found that 94 percent of Internet sites did not require a prescription, ("You've Got Drugs!—Pushers on the Internet," a white paper released by The National Center on Addiction and Substance Abuse at Columbia University and Beau Dietl and Associates, retrieved from Internet 01/17/05 at *http://alcoholism.about.com/cs/prescription/a/?once=true&*).

Prescription drug addiction includes common pain relievers such as Vicodin, codeine, OxyContin, Darvon, Dilaudid, and Demerol. These prescription pain relievers are opiate derivatives and act in the body similar to heroin and morphine so in addition to blocking pain, they also produce a "euphoria" that is highly addictive. Most prescription drug users begin taking the drug to help alleviate emotional or physical pain. The user may continue to crave the high after the pain has stopped. Tolerance develops quickly and the patient will eventually require larger amounts of the drug. Doctors often give warnings regarding the potential for addiction, but patients may still find themselves addicted. Mixing alcohol and pills is also common. The effects produce a high that is superior to either of the drugs used alone. However, combining prescription drugs with alcohol can be fatal.

Prescription drug users often justify the use of the drug, stating they are only relieving pain. It has less of a stigma than the use of other illegal non-prescription drugs. Family members typically don't understand that the addiction is just as powerful and damaging. Treatment is the same for prescription drug addiction as for other drug and alcohol. The overuse of prescription drugs causes multiple health problems and can result in death.

The following list includes some of the more commonly used illicit and prescription drugs with a brief description.

Cocaine and Crack

These come from the leaves of the coca plant. Cocaine is usually snorted through the nostrils or injected intravenously. Crack is inhaled, giving it a more rapid onset. Both stimulants cause an increase in energy, intense euphoria, clearer thinking, and a positive mood. At high doses, users experience a "rush" which is an intense but short feeling of euphoria and pleasure. Users may take high doses repeatedly for days at a time. During these "runs," users hardly sleep and eat. They often stop when they run out of the drug, then sleep for long periods (24-48 hours), and eat large quantities of food. High doses can cause psychotic and paranoid behavior including hallucinations, delusions, and violence. Personality changes can include depression, paranoia, mood swings, anxiety, hostility, aggression, and defensiveness. Dependency can develop rapidly. Some people initially use cocaine to lose weight, increase their energy, or increase productivity.

Amphetamines

These are also stimulants, but they are longer lasting than both cocaine and crack so they are taken fewer times a day. Illegal amphetamines include speed, uppers, bennies, and black beauties. Amphetamines increase brain activity and energy, decrease appetite, and cause euphoria. Users typically don't sleep for days. People often ingest alcohol or other sedatives with amphetamines to reduce the nervousness they feel. Dependency on the drug develops very quickly when injected. Some people start taking amphetamines to lose weight. Side effects are numerous: irritability, aggressiveness, anxiousness, paranoia, and eventually heart problems, hallucinations, tremors, and permanent neurological damage.

Crystal Methamphetamine

This is a popular and powerful stimulant easily made in home labs from common ingredients such as over-the-counter cold and asthma medications containing ephedrine or pseudoephedrine, antifreeze, battery acid, drain cleaner, red phosphorus, hydrochloric acid, and lye. Nicknames include "ice," "speed," "meth," "crank," and "glass." It is highly addictive. Side effects include stroke, weight loss, and psychotic, erratic, agitated, or violent behavior.

Cannabinoids

These come from the cannabis plant and include marijuana and hashish. Marijuana comes from the upper leaves, tops, and stems of the plant and hashish comes from the dried resin on the leaves.

Both are usually smoked. Physiological effects include bloodshot eyes, increased appetite, dry mouth, and increased heart rate. The "high" is characterized by feelings of well-being, laughter, and a dream-like state. Occasionally, users experience hallucinations, anxiety, and paranoia. Chronic use can cause bronchitis, apathy, fatigue, decreased motivation, depression, anxiety, and impaired judgment. Long-term use is sometimes associated with learning problems and decreased memory. Marijuana is often used with alcohol and other drugs.

Hallucinogens

Some common forms include LSD, Ecstasy, morning glory, psilocybin, mescaline, and DMT. All cause the user to have hallucinations. People don't usually use the drug more than several times a week but still experience negative effects. Many of the hallucinogens are long-acting and require days to come down completely. Users can have "bad trips" where they experience paranoia and panic. They can also experience anxiety, depression, and poor judgment. Flashbacks are re-experiencing the hallucinations after the drug use has stopped. The flashbacks may or may not cause psychological distress.

Phencyclidine or PCP

This is a synthetic drug that causes euphoria and a feeling of unreality. It can also cause psychotic behavior, extreme excitation, catatonic states (posturing for lengthy time periods), mood changes, aggression, impaired judgment, disorientation, slurred speech, loss of coordination of muscle movements, and medical problems. People with dependence usually take it several times a day. Ketamine, also known as Special K, K, or kitkat is similar to PCP.

Opiates

They include natural and synthetic drugs either similar to opium or derived from opium. They include heroin, morphine, codeine, Demerol, Darvon, Vicodin, OxyContin, and Methadone. Opiate use results in feeling euphoria and relaxation, pain relief, reduction of fear and anxiety, drowsiness, dizziness, slurred speech, impaired judgment, and a detachment from reality. Users who inject or smoke opiates experience a rush, described as so pleasurable that users want to experience it again. Addiction occurs quickly. Withdrawal is less intense than alcohol or barbiturates and is not life threatening.

In the United States, methadone is sometimes given to heroin addicts as a maintenance drug or to reduce withdrawal symptoms. Some users continue to use the methadone for many years. For those who want to be clean, the dosage is reduced slowly to decrease withdrawal.

Central Nervous System Depressants

These are primarily designed to reduce anxiety or cause sleep by slowing normal brain function. They include alcohol, barbiturates, and benzodiazepines. Prescription drugs include Valium, Xanax, Halcion, Restoril, Ativan, Ambiem, Librium, and Nembutal. The primary effect of these drugs is to induce a state of relaxation. These drugs are sometimes used in conjunction with cocaine or amphetamines to moderate the stimulant effect. Using depressants with alcohol can slow the heart rate and breathing and possibly result in death. Strong physiological dependency is typical for many of these drugs. Tolerance also occurs, requiring more of the drug to get the same effect.

Now that you have some background, let's look at the situation in which a spouse is the substance abuser.

Helping the Wife of a Substance Abuser

The woman you are dealing with is most likely overwhelmed with a myriad of problems. She is fearful, obsessed, worried, angry, guilty, confused, frustrated, lonely, ashamed, and hopeless. She has prayed and hoped, been disappointed, and prayed some more. She may wonder if God even cares.

She may feel guilty for even telling you about her husband, thinking that she is betraying him by speaking badly of him. She is probably embarrassed to tell you how out of control she sometimes gets. She will worry about what you and others will think of her.

In the absence of an understanding of substance abuse, some people might be tempted to give her simple answers, like: "Trust God," "Love your husband," "Pray," or "Submit to your husband and God will take care of it." She has heard those answers before and become more discouraged.

Unfortunately, the church sometimes presents an inaccurate and limited view of submission that suggests to a woman that all she has to do is submit to her husband for God to bless her marriage. Inferred is that she cannot say no to him or set healthy limits and boundaries.

Use these principles in helping the women whose husbands are users.

1. Understand scriptural truths
The woman needs to understand that she can say no to her husband; that she does not have to submit to him if the request causes her to disobey God, hurt her children, violate her conscience, or hurt her husband by continuing to enable his addiction. Acts 5:29 set this precedent when Peter responded to the authorities telling them not to preach the gospel, stating, "We must obey God rather than men!"

The woman married to a substance abuser needs to understand that it is her responsibility to stand up against the destructive force of alcohol and drugs that are wreaking havoc in her marriage, life, husband's life, and children's lives. She needs to know that submission to a man who is not even loving his own body can be dangerous. His decisions are not necessarily good for the marriage, himself, her, or the family.

We read in the Book of Esther that Queen Vashti's drunken husband King Xerxes summoned her and wanted her to parade herself before the men at his drunken feast. She refused, even though he got angry and it was unacceptable in her day to refuse his request (Esth. 1:4-12).

The woman needs to understand that it may be more difficult to stand up for what is right than to allow the addiction to continue passively without taking a stand. First Peter 3:17 reminds us that it is better to suffer for doing good than for doing evil. Ephesians 5:11 also says, "Have nothing to do with fruitless deeds of darkness, but rather expose them" (NIV). Help her understand that persevering and long-suffering do not mean she should passively endure the situation without confronting, setting boundaries, and protecting herself and her children. It is important that she realize she can persevere best by learning how to use a tough love approach.

As Christians, we are supposed to bear good fruit, including the fruit of the Spirit (Gal. 5:22-25) and fruit from our godly lives. Addictions produce bad fruit—not only by the addict but also often by the non-addict's response to the addict. A woman has to evaluate whether her action or inaction is producing the fruit of righteousness in her husband, herself, and her children. Is it producing sin, envy, arguing, anger, resentment, brokenness, despair, and destructive encounters? Or, is it planting the seeds of righteousness by doing things that increase goodness, peace, repentance, accountability, godliness, kindness, and love?

First Peter 3:1-4 reminds women married to unsaved husbands that they should not nag them to get them saved, but rather live quiet and respectable lives that testify to their faith. This is sometimes incorrectly applied to women in difficult marriages, giving them the impression they should not say anything to their husbands about addictions or abuse. This verse was not intended to prevent a woman from being able to deal effectively with real problems.

Galatians 6:7-9 says, "Do not be deceived: God cannot be mocked. A man reaps what he sows. The one who sows to please his sinful nature, from that nature will reap destruction; the one who sows to please the Spirit, from the Spirit will reap eternal life. Let us not become weary in doing good, for at the proper time we will reap a harvest if we do not give up" (NIV). Remind her that God holds her husband accountable for his actions and that he should bear the consequences for them; not her. This will help her not to enable him.

She also needs to know that God cares about her and accepts her just as she is and that there is hope for her future.

> "For I know the plans I have for you"—this is the LORD's
> declaration—"plans for your welfare, not for disaster, to give
> you a future and a hope."
> Jeremiah 29:11

2. Reach out
She has probably suffered alone for a long time. She is reaching out to you for support. Refer her to Twelve Step groups like Al-Anon, Nar-Anon, or the equivalent Christian program, counselors, and other church members who have experienced similar problems. Hearing from others who have experienced similar situations and are now living better lives gives her hope.

Tell her it is OK for her to get help, even if her husband tells her not to or gets angry. If she needs financial help, rides to meetings, a babysitter, or any other resources, consider supplying them, as long as it helps her to get better, not to bail out her husband.

3. Change herself, not him
She has spent a tremendous amount of energy trying to change her husband and get him to stop drinking or using drugs. She has obsessively focused on her husband and not on herself. Her life, like the addict's, is now unmanageable and

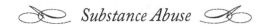

out of control. She needs to realize that she has no power to change her husband but that she does have the ability and responsibility to change herself and her reactions and actions, thereby changing her life and possibly her husband and marriage. Help her to understand that no matter what her husband says, she cannot make him want to get sober and that she did not cause his addiction.

4. Detach with love

The typical wife is attached so strongly to her husband that she lets the addiction dominate her life. She spends her energy covering up for him, protecting him, reacting to him, and letting him determine her moods and choices. Detachment helps her to separate herself from him in a healthy way. The addict needs to experience the consequences of his addiction. If he does not, the chances that he will get help are slim. So, detachment teaches her to stop enabling him.

The wife also needs to separate herself emotionally, physically, mentally, and spiritually from her husband's choices so that she can stop reacting to him. He uses her reactions to blame her for his substance abuse. She needs to learn to detach herself so he cannot control how she feels and reacts. When she stops reacting to him negatively, she will feel less guilty and responsible for his addiction and see it clearly as his problem. She can still treat him with compassion, courtesy, and love, while holding him accountable for his actions. Help her to see how she is enabling him, why she needs to stop, and that she needs to quit reacting to him.

5. Nurture herself

It is easy for a woman married to an addict to ignore her own needs while responding to the various crises and problems that arise repeatedly. She may even believe that doing things for herself is selfish. And, the addict sometimes tells her that it is, since he expects life to center on him and his needs. This woman needs to learn to value herself by taking care of herself mentally, emotionally, spiritually, and physically. If she does not strengthen and stabilize herself, she will not have the ability to make choices that improve her family.

6. Face her fears

Fear is a natural reaction to perceived danger. The woman married to an addict lives with many fearful situations: potential arrests and accidents, arguments, financial deficits, threats, divorce, loss of jobs, problems with the children, people finding out, and possibly marital infidelity. She begins to worry about the future, living with "What if" continually on her mind. Some of the threats are real and others are projections into the future. She needs to be able to identify and share her fears, do whatever she can today about them, and then turn over the rest to God. Help her to identify her fears, see if there is anything she can do, and trust God with the rest. (We'll look at some of her fears in the section on family dynamics.)

7. Speak the truth in love

Women married to addicts doubt themselves. They've lived with denial and lies for so long that they have become confused with what the truth is. The first thing they need to do is to know the truth about their lives by letting go of denial and self-doubt. Then they have to be able to speak the truth. Women have either passively accepted things or continually argued. Speaking the truth is different than both of those extremes. She must be willing to speak the truth but not by attacking her husband. Help her by validating the truth about her life and by helping her learn to speak the truth in love.

8. Set boundaries

Boundaries are not meant to tell this woman's husband what he cannot do. Rather they set parameters for what she will and will not do. She has no power to make her husband do anything. The only thing she can do is to decide what she will do with his choices.

This list isn't exhaustive, but it will give you an idea of some of the issues this woman faces. Will she ...
- stay with him if he uses drugs in front of the children or in the home?
- let him drive the children in the car if he is under the influence?
- ride with him?
- buy his alcohol?
- go to work if the bills aren't paid?
- give him her paycheck if he spends his irresponsibly?
- argue with him while he's under the influence?
- tolerate physical or emotional abuse?

These questions and many more are all boundary issues that she will have to decide for herself. Because her husband has probably told her that he will either leave or not respect them, her boundaries initially will be weak and she will be fearful of setting them. It is then that she will have to decide whether separation and possibly divorce is a consideration. Help her to see that it is important for her to identify and set boundaries to protect herself and her children and to make a stand for what is right in her home.

9. Make her children a priority

Children are greatly affected by addiction. A wife and mother desperately tries to prevent the children from finding out, but they usually already know something is wrong. She cannot prevent their being affected, but she can make it better by validating their emotions, protecting them from abuse, telling them age-appropriate truth rather than covering up, modeling coping skills, meeting their needs, providing stability, and disciplining them when necessary.

10. Enter God's rest

Living with addictions is like life on an endless roller coaster ride. Sometimes things aren't so bad; but then they get bad again, and the cycle continues.

Positive change doesn't happen quickly, and it may require painful losses for the addict to hit bottom. Even sobriety adds stress, change, and relational and financial pressures. Like addicts, women need to learn to live one day at a time rather than projecting into the future. They need to learn to do what is right today and trust God with the outcome.

You can read more about these in *10 Lifesaving Principles for Women in Difficult Marriages* by Karla Downing, Beacon Hill Press, Kansas City, 2003.

Family Dynamics

As the disease of substance abuse progresses, relationships deteriorate. Addicts care less about other people and more about their addiction and themselves. They lie about their using and become defensive and hostile, especially when their spouses try to talk to them about the substance abuse and any problems it might be causing.

Denial is an integral part of addiction. Addicts refuse to believe they have a problem until they are ready to do something about it. They minimize the evidence, blaming the problems that occur as a result of their using on others and circumstances. Or they may rationalize it by saying something like:
"Maybe I do drink too much, but then who wouldn't with the stress I have?"
"I can stop anytime—I just don't want to right now."
"I only need it to relax."
"I'm taking it for pain. What's wrong with that?"

Families often struggle trying to figure out if their family member is truly a drug addict or alcoholic. It doesn't really matter. If someone else's drinking or drug use bothers them, the person probably has a problem, and they have to figure out how to deal with the situation.

Drug use and alcoholism affect the family in predictable ways. Because you will be dealing with women who struggle with drug or alcohol use by their husbands, for the sake of simplicity the following description will use the pronoun "he" for the addict and "she" for the spouse. However, when the woman is the drug addict or alcoholic, the husband experiences the same things.

Fears

With both drugs and alcohol, this woman worries and has real fears. The following are written as if the woman is saying them to help you relate as if she asks them out loud.
- What if he gets arrested? We can't pay the bills if he loses his job.
- What if he has to go to court? Court and attorney costs are high.
- What if the children find the substance, accidentally ingest it, or just find out about it?
- What do I tell friends, family members, or neighbors?

- If I don't let him use at home, will he drive under the influence? I'd feel guilty and couldn't stop worrying.
- What if he gets hurt? What if he hurts others?
- I worry about his health; it's deteriorating.
- Who is he getting the drugs from? Do they pose a danger to my family?
- Drugs are expensive. How much money is he really spending? Our basic needs aren't even being met.
- I don't want to have the alcohol in the house at all. Can I ask him not to bring it home? But, if the alcohol isn't at the house, will he go somewhere else to get it?
- I don't want his drinking friends here at the house. Can I say no? Where will he go to drink then?
- Should I go with him when he drinks to take care of him?
- Will life ever be different? Will it ever be better?

In addition to worry and fear, this wife is angry. She's angry that her husband continues to use and refuses to get help. She's also angry that he denies he has a problem.

Her Behaviors

To cope with the situation falling apart around her, she begins to get sick too. As she sees this growing problem, she attempts to hold the family together. To do this, she begins to deny that the problem is as bad as it is. She does this because she desperately wants to believe that everything is OK.

She covers up for the addict so that the family doesn't suffer the consequences. She may borrow money or get a job to cover the bills. She may lie to his boss when he misses work and make excuses to friends and family so they won't know how bad it really is. She doesn't want the children to know their dad is an addict so she makes excuses to them for why he doesn't show up for their special events or come home for dinner. She tells them he isn't feeling well, not that he is hung-over or intoxicated.

She cleans up the messes in the house from the arguments and his getting sick. She tries to control the drinking and using. She hides his keys, pours out alcohol, searches for drugs and alcohol, monitors his intake, and "walks on eggshells" to try to keep the peace so he won't use. She has become an enabler. An enabler allows the addict to continue to drink or use without feeling the consequences of his behavior. Enablers prolong the addiction because an addict won't usually hit bottom until he feels the pain from his actions.

While she is covering up and holding things together, she is desperately trying to change the addict. She pleads, begs, explains, threatens, rages, cries, and nags him. She repeatedly tells him how he is falling short and how he is hurting himself, her, and the children. The more he denies, the harder she tries to explain. She becomes obsessed with trying to get him to see the problem, looking for the magic words that will open his eyes. It doesn't work—it only makes her life unmanageable in the process.

The addict blames those around him for his addiction and its consequences. His blame is an excuse not to take personal responsibility. He believes it is his wife's fault that he drinks or uses. He may even pick a fight or provoke her by pushing her in ways that he knows will make her react, so he can say he has to go out and drink or use. He blames her for the financial problems. It isn't his expenditures or lost income from missing work, it is her overspending and mismanagement. She may be reacting to her husband, arguing, and emotionally out of control frequently herself. She may be yelling at the children. When she looks at herself, she realizes how out of control she is and comes to believe that it is her fault. She believes that she should be able to hold things together and that she should be able to figure out how to fix her husband.

An Elephant in the Living Room

Alcoholism has been referred to as the elephant in the living room. No one talks about it, but they know it is there. They step around it and adapt to it but don't talk about how they feel about it. Everyone knows how to adjust their actions not to disturb the elephant.

These families live by the rules of dysfunctional families:
  • Don't talk.
  • Don't feel.
  • Don't trust.
  • Don't rock the boat.
  • Don't be selfish.

Whether it's alcoholism or drug abuse, the addict's family knows what they have to do to survive. When one member chooses to do things that put it at risk, the others have to do things that balance it out.

Children

"Children find ways to cope with the unpredictability, instability, and painful emotions to bring order and balance to their lives as much as possible. One way they do this is by adopting roles in the family. Some children become overly responsible, taking care of their parents, siblings, and the household. Some become super-good, attempting to be loved for their achievements. Others become invisible so they don't add more demands to the overwhelmed family system. Some develop problems in an attempt to get the family to look at the truth or to take the focus off the real issues, allowing the parents the opportunity to unite to deal with the child's difficulty. Children also take on the role of the peacemaker, attempting to resolve disputes," (*When Love Hurts: 10 Principles to Transform Difficult Relationships* by Karla Downing, 2004, p. 34-35.).

No way around it, children are affected. They are aware of the problems, sense the fear, hear the arguments, and feel the family pain and confusion. They know what they see and feel and then when their feelings and perceptions are not validated, they get confused and doubt themselves. They worry about what will happen to the family. They may even feel guilty that they cannot fix it. Sometimes they are abused by parents who deal with them in anger because the parents are either under the influence of drugs and/or alcohol or are emotionally overwhelmed with problems.

Wife Is Sick Too

No matter what, the wife of the alcoholic or addict has to realize that she, too, has become sick and so has the family. She now needs help as much as the addict. She will learn that she did not cause her husband to drink or use drugs. She cannot control his drinking or drug use. She cannot make him stop, but she does have power over her own life and that is where she needs to focus.

Helping the Woman Who Is a Substance Abuser

Some of the women you minister to will have substance abuse problems themselves. If they come to you asking for help, you can offer support in the following ways.

1. Refer her to rehabilitation programs or Twelve Step programs like Alcoholics Anonymous, Narcotics Anonymous, or a Christian Twelve Step program. See the Resource List at the end of this chapter for specific information on some of these.

2. Help her to see her addiction as a disease that she needs help with rather than simply as a moral failing or sin. Show her plenty of grace and assure her that God has a plan and will help her overcome her addiction.

3. Connect her with a recovered addict. This person might be a member of your church. Whether or not she is a member, be sure that this woman has recovered and is living a healthy Christian life.

If You Approach the Woman

If the woman doesn't come to you but you have concerns about her drug or alcohol abuse, you have a different situation. Nevertheless, it's important to reach out to her.

1. Be honest with her about your concerns and observations. You don't have to decide if she is a drug addict or alcoholic; instead, tell her why you are concerned. Don't condemn her. Let her know you care. Most importantly, let her know how much God loves and cares for her.

2. If you work with her, don't cover for her absences or mistakes or make excuses for poor work. This is called enabling and will prolong her addiction.

3. If you suspect she might be neglecting or abusing her children, talk to her about it. If she doesn't make changes, tell her you will call Child Protective Services (CPS). An interim step may be to talk with her husband or one of her relatives or close friends and try to arrange for someone to take the children. As a minister or church worker, you may be legally required to report child abuse and neglect to CPS. Check with CPS to see what your state's laws require you to do. It may seem cruel to take the children away from her, but remember, she has to face the consequences of her addiction before she will quit. Most importantly, children are innocent victims and deserve protection.

4. Don't pay her bills or bail her out of financial difficulties.

5. If she does not get help after talking to you, share your concerns with her family. Give them information about addiction or Twelve Step programs for them including Al-Anon, Nar-Anon, or Christian programs such as Celebrate Recovery.

6. If you are in a position of authority, you may have the difficult decision of asking her to step down from a leadership, employment, or volunteer position in your church or organization. Not doing it because you feel sorry for her means you are enabling her. You can ask her to step down until she recovers and then under certain conditions ask her to return. The decision whether to ask her to step down will depend on what position she holds and the severity and type of her addiction. The Americans with Disability Act has specific requirements that employers have to follow to accommodate some alcoholic employees. Under certain conditions, alcoholism is a disability and you are limited from firing someone for it. Current illegal drug addiction is not considered a disability, but you cannot let someone go for past drug use. Many other specific details must be observed, so seek legal advice first.

7. Offer to help her with practical things that support her recovery:
   • Help with her children's needs while she is at Twelve Step meetings or rehabilitation.
   • Give her rides to her rehabilitation.

8. Intervening. Should you call the police if you know she is driving under the influence, keep her from driving by intervening or taking her keys, or report illegal drug possession? While in some circumstances this is appropriate, it is generally better to let natural consequences take over. Al-Anon recommends that members not prevent a crisis or cause a crisis. If you do decide to get involved, make sure it doesn't cause you to cover up or take over her responsibilities or result in legal difficulties for you or your church or ministry.

9. You can't make her see she has a problem. She will stay in denial until she is ready to admit that using drugs or alcohol is more painful than not using. Be patient and honest with her. Don't cover for her in the process.

Treatment

You have probably heard that addicts have to hit bottom to quit using. Hitting bottom is when users get low enough to want to stop and realize they need help to do it. Addicts can hit bottom through a tragedy such as the loss of a job, family, marriage, health, or money; through an intervention; or by deciding to change on their own. An intervention is where family and friends confront the addict together with what he or she is doing to him- or herself and how the behavior is affecting each of them. Regardless of how they get there, addicts have to want to live without the substance. No one can make an addict want that. Until using feels worse than stopping, they won't stop.

In some ways, addicts are better off when using than when sober. They are less uncomfortable when anesthetized because alcohol and drugs provide some relief or escape from the negative emotions and craving they experience when not under the influence. Somehow, they have to see that even the initial withdrawal period and subsequent experiencing of difficult emotions and craving are more desirable than the benefits they get from using. This is often accomplished through experiencing a significant amount of negative consequences related to the addiction.

The goal is to help the addict stop as early in the disease as possible. Many addicts enter treatment out of coercion. Treatment teams then have to try to change their motivation from having to abstain to wanting to abstain. Recovery also needs to focus on changing the addictive thinking: The addict needs to be less self-centered, handle emotions and stress better, take responsibility for his or her actions, let go of resentments, and improve self-worth.

The first thing treatment has to address is detoxification. Physical detoxification is the withdrawal from a substance by stopping the substance completely and abruptly, systematically decreasing the dose, or by giving other substances to control the withdrawal symptoms. Physical withdrawal from drugs can be as short as one day and as long as several weeks. Symptoms vary and include craving, sleeplessness, excessive sleep, anxiety, sweating, nausea, vomiting, diarrhea, dizziness, convulsions, irritability, changes in heart rate, restlessness, tremors, agitation, chills, fever, cramps, delirium, and hallucinations. Milder withdrawal can include anxiety, panic, and decreased memory and concentration. Withdrawal from heavy and prolonged alcohol use and some drugs can be life threatening, requiring medical management of symptoms.

The body also needs to be cleansed from the toxic buildup of chemicals. This is often done through good nutrition and detoxification techniques. Having the addict detoxify in a controlled environment in which the drug isn't accessible increases the chance that he or she will not use during the intense craving. Withdrawal can be dangerous and at times requires medical management. Other times, depending on the severity of the addiction and withdrawal, the addict may not even need a structured detoxification environment; simply making a decision to quit and attending a recovery program or Twelve Step meetings may be enough.

Payment for treatment programs varies. Some county-run programs are free. Programs can be non-profit or for-profit. Many have sliding fee scales that vary according to income. Some insurance policies will pay for treatment. Some employers have an employee assistance program that refers employees to treatment programs paid for by the employer. Some programs take payments from the state for people enrolled in healthcare programs for low-income families and dependent or disabled individuals. Some churches offer rehabilitation programs. The Salvation Army has free residential programs. Many programs require the addict to be clean or sober before entering the program. Often addicts are required to attend Twelve Step program meetings.

Inpatient treatment involves the addict staying night and day and focusing totally on recovery. Treatment includes medical management of detoxification, education, counseling, and group meetings. This treatment is expensive, but some insurance policies and employers pay for it. Inpatient treatment needs to be followed by aftercare groups that offer the addict support when they return to their lives.

Outpatient treatment is less expensive and has two types: In a day treatment program, the addict goes to treatment all day and then goes home at night. Treatment is fairly intense. In other outpatient programs, the addict works, lives at home, and goes to meetings several times a week. In both types, the meetings consist of lectures, films, group therapy, family therapy, and Twelve Step group meetings. The negative of outpatient treatment is that the dropout rate is higher because the addict has to return to the program voluntarily. Achieving sobriety is also more difficult because the addict has to deal with family and life problems while enduring the initial difficulties of abstinence.

Some addicts go to a halfway house or sober living home after achieving sobriety. These do not offer structured treatment for the addicts. Instead, the addicts are responsible for voluntarily participating in activities that support sobriety. They may work at their jobs during the day and go back at night. They learn to live responsibly with others and share tasks in the home. Living with other newly sober addicts keeps the focus on recovery. The halfway house allows the addict time to readjust and focus on sobriety before going back to the family or social environments that pose additional stress at a time that the addict is desperately trying to adjust to living without drugs and/or alcohol.

Some programs use Disulfiram (Antabuse) to help the addict stay off alcohol. When the alcoholic takes the Antabuse and drinks alcohol, it results in headache, flushing, nausea, vomiting, dizziness, light-headedness, and tachycardia. This aversion therapy helps some alcoholics make it through the initial withdrawal period when craving is high. Other drugs help to reduce craving.

Psychotherapy or counseling can be an important part of the addict's recovery, but it is not enough to achieve sobriety initially. Some counselors will not see clients who are actively using drugs or alcohol. Family therapy can be helpful to repair the damage from alcohol or drug use and to help the family adjust to sobriety. It can also help the family learn to communicate effectively and manage problems. It is critical to have professional support if the addiction is related to an underlying mental disorder such as bipolar disease, depression, post-traumatic stress disorder, schizophrenia, or anxiety.

Twelve-Step Programs

Alcoholics Anonymous was started in 1935 by Bill Wilson and Dr. Bob Smith, two alcoholics who found sobriety through the help of the Oxford Group. This group, founded by Sam Shoemaker, was an evangelical, Christ-centered organization that ran a rescue mission in New York City. It was there that Bill and Bob were introduced to the scriptural principles that not only helped them to overcome their alcoholism but were the foundation of the Twelve Step program. *(Steps to a New Beginning* by Shoemaker, Minirth, Fowler, Newman, and Carder, 1993, Thomas Nelson Publishers.)

The Twelve Steps are based on scriptural principles that include 1) the idea that addicts and their family members are powerless over the addiction; 2) help from God is necessary to change oneself; 3) confession of sins; 4) the need to make amends; and 5) the need to reach out to help others. Alcoholics Anonymous knew that a reliance on God was the reason for their success: "Remember that we deal with alcohol—cunning, baffling, powerful! Without help it is too much for us. But there is One who has all power—that One is God," (Alcoholics Anonymous, pp. 58-59). The Twelve Steps refers to God as "God" and a "Power greater than ourselves," rather than to Jesus Christ. Some Christians find that offensive. Others understand that an effective program needs to draw all people, rather than exclude some, and that many find Jesus Christ during their sobriety.

In 1950, Lois, Bill W.'s wife, brought together the wives of alcoholics and formed Al-Anon. In 1957, Alateen was formed for the children of alcoholics. Since then other Twelve Step groups have formed to support other addictions and their family members, including Narcotics Anonymous for drug addicts and Nar-Anon for their families. Some churches have started their own recovery groups where the Higher Power is identified as Jesus Christ.

Twelve Step groups for addicts are based on the belief that an addict suffers from a disease that affects his or her body, mind, and spirit. This "disease" will result in death or insanity if untreated. Labeling alcoholism or drug addiction merely as "sin" implies that all the addict has to do is confess and stop. It is critical that addicts understand that they are truly powerless over the addiction and that without the help of God and others, they will continue to use. Addicts are responsible for their actions when they drink or use drugs, and for the choice to take the first drink or drug; however, they have to see the disease as bigger than just willpower. Looking at the unmanageability of their lives as a result of their disease is all the evidence they need. They have tried many times to quit and have failed, even though they were sincere when they made the promises.

Twelve Step groups encourage sponsorship. A sponsor is someone who has had more time in the program before becoming a mentor. A sponsor and sponsoree talk about personal situations that come up, and the sponsor helps the sponsoree apply the program's steps. It is also a way of being accountable.

Twelve Step groups offer help for addicts desiring to get clean. When an addict calls a local county service office of Alcoholics Anonymous or Narcotics Anonymous, they will send a seasoned member out on the "Twelve Step Call." This member will help the addict get to either a meeting or a detox center/treatment program, depending on which is necessary. This member becomes a temporary sponsor to help the addict get sober or clean.

Sobriety

Most addicts have to continue to attend meetings to stay sober. "Working the program" involves continuing to work the Steps with a sponsor for accountability and applying the Steps and principles to one's life. It also involves working the Twelfth Step by interacting with other addicts, helping them to get sober. Bill W. and Dr. Bob knew that this was a crucial part of the alcoholic's need to be reminded that he or she cannot drink or use again.

The Twelve Steps help the addict to stay sober, but they also help them improve the spiritual, emotional, mental, and relational dimensions of their lives. The family also needs treatment because if the family doesn't change, the addict will often go back to using or the family will break up.

Sobriety has its own problems and adjustments. Addicts go to recovery meetings and are frequently away from their families. They are dealing with emotions and feelings they may not have dealt with before. They may be moody and edgy at first from not having the substance. They may not have been involved in day-to-day decisions and child rearing before but now have opinions about how things should be, requiring conflict resolution.

Many spouses resent the changes addicts want in the family, even though they were angry before that they weren't involved. It is also important that spouses don't feel responsible for the addict's maintenance of sobriety. They are the only ones who can choose to stay sober. The family has to be honest and real about their issues. The spouse, who spent his or her entire life focusing on getting the addict sober, has lost his or her role and has to find a new one. Change is stressful, even when it is good change. In addition, if the addict is still emotionally drunk, as with the case of a dry drunk personality, the spouse may not get relief from the difficulties. Some addicts may even be more difficult to deal with, as they are trying to deal with life without the anesthetizing substance that allowed them to cope. Sobriety doesn't erase personality problems, relationship issues, or character defects.

"By the time sobriety comes to the one we love, our heads are still full of the remembrances of watchful waiting; our emotions are packed with anger and leftover resentments; our spirits are weighed down by the broken promises and the absence of trust. Almost everything about us has been altered by our reactions to drinking situations. These effects on our behavior, so often subtle and insidious, were years in the making and won't disappear just because someone else stops drinking" (*Living with Sobriety: Another Beginning*, Al-Anon Family Group Headquarters, Inc., New York, 1979, p. 5). That is why the spouse also needs recovery.

Relapse

Alcoholism and drug addiction are lifetime diseases. Most addicts cannot control their use even after a long period of sobriety. Even when they have been clean and dry for years, one use allows them to quickly pick up where they left off in the progression of the disease. The addict has to know that avoiding the first drink or drug is imperative. Many addicts have stories of being sober for years and then using again for years after allowing themselves to slip.

Yet, relapse for the newly recovering addict is common. Most make multiple attempts at getting sober before they finally are able to. The spouse fears relapse. However, sometimes relapse can be the very thing that teaches an addict that he or she cannot use. It doesn't have to mean that the addict reverts back to where he or she was before sobriety. Twelve Step programs use the slogan "One Day at a Time" to encourage the addict to stay sober for today. Addicts have to understand they have the ability to decide whether to take the first drink or drug, but after its first use the addiction takes over and they become powerless over it.

Changes in addicts' thinking and actions happen before they choose to drink or use again. They may stop going to meetings, getting counseling, or talking to sponsors. They begin to question whether they are truly addicts and unable to use or drink. They may go back to the places or people with whom they used or drank. Then, they give in to the thinking and use or drink again.

Certain things present a threat to sobriety: guilt, holidays, unhealthy relationships, hunger, high-pressure situations, anger, lack of sleep, loneliness, self-pity, over-confidence, arrogance, or resentment. The addict needs to manage these problems to minimize using again. The newly sober alcoholic or clean addict needs to avoid places and people that remind him or her of alcohol or drugs. The brain associates places and faces with memories of the good feelings associated with being under the influence. When the senses take in the familiar places, it will also pull up the familiar feelings and increase the addict's craving for the substance.

The responsibility for sobriety and relapse belongs to the addict. No one can make someone else stay sober or clean. The family doesn't need to walk on eggshells to make sure that the addict doesn't relapse. They need to live their own lives.

Recommended Resources

10 Lifesaving Principles for Women in Difficult Marriages by Karla Downing, Beacon Hill Press of Kansas City, 2003.

When Love Hurts: 10 Principles to Transform Difficult Relationships by Karla Downing, Beacon Hill Press of Kansas City, 2004.

Getting Them Sober—You Can Help! by Toby Rice Drews, Recovery Communications, 1998.

Quitting for Good: A Christ-Centered Approach to Nicotine Dependency by Frances McClain, B&H Publishing Group, 1995.

Twelve Step Organizations

The following contacts can direct you to the nearest local service with lists of meetings in your area.

Alcoholics Anonymous World Service Office
For alcoholics
(212) 870-3400
www.aa.org

Cocaine Anonymous World Services
For cocaine addicts
(310) 559-5833
www.ca.org

Co-Anon Family Groups
For families of cocaine addicts
(800) 898-9985 or (520) 513-5028
www.co-anon.org

Al-Anon Family Groups
For families of alcoholics and includes Alateen for teens
(888) 425-2666
www.al-anon.alateen.org

Celebrate Recovery
www.celebraterecovery.com (check for a group near you)

Narcotics Anonymous
For drug addicts
(818) 773-9999
www.na.org

Nar-Anon Family Groups Headquarters
For families of drug addicts
(800) 477-6291 or (310) 534-8188
http://nar-anon.org/index.html

Overcomers Outreach
Christian recovery for addicts and their families
(800) 310-3001
www.overcomersoutreach.org

Treatment Programs

Substance Abuse and Mental Health Services Administration
(800) 662-4357
www.findtreatment.samhsa.gov
24-hour referral to alcohol and drug prevention and treatment programs and services. Spanish spoken. Free Services. Serves all of the United States.

Local service offices for Alcoholics Anonymous and Narcotics Anonymous can help get the addict to either meetings or a treatment center, depending on what he or she needs. Either give the addict the number or make the call for them.

Terms

Be familiar with the following terms that are affiliated with substance abuse.

Addict: a man or woman whose life is controlled by drugs, alcohol, or any other substance or behavior.

Alcoholic: someone whose drinking negatively, regularly, and increasingly affects any aspect of life: physical, mental, emotional, social, relational, or spiritual and who cannot stop drinking.

Alcoholics Anonymous (AA): The first Twelve Step group started by Bill Wilson and Dr. Bob Smith in 1935 for alcoholics.

Al-Anon: The Twelve Step program for family members of alcoholics.

Alateen: The Twelve Step program for children of alcoholics.

Blackout: when a person under the influence appears to be functioning normally but later doesn't remember anything.

Detoxification: Also called detox. Physical detox is the withdrawal from a substance by stopping the substance completely and abruptly, by systematically decreasing the dose, or by giving other substances to control the withdrawal symptoms.

Drug: a substance that alters the physiology of the body but is not a food or nutrient. Includes both prescription and illegal "street" forms.

Dry drunk: someone who experiences the same irrational thought processes and moods that the addict experiences under the influence without being intoxicated. It refers to mood changes and thinking processes rather than physical symptoms.

DTs: abbreviation for delirium tremens. It involves seeing, hearing, or feeling things that aren't real, such as bugs or snakes crawling on the body. Occurs when an addict is trying to get off dependence on a substance.

Enable: actions that allow the addict to continue to drink or use without feeling the consequences of his or her behavior. Enablers prolong the addiction because an addict won't usually hit bottom until he or she feels the pain from their actions.

Grandiosity: This is when the addict has an exaggerated sense of his or her own importance, abilities, knowledge, accomplishments, or significance.

Hangover: mild withdrawal symptoms that can be relieved by consuming more alcohol.

Intervention: when family and friends confront the addict together with what he or she is doing to himself or herself and how it is affecting each of them.

Inpatient treatment: an addict stays night and day at a treatment facility and focuses totally on recovery.

Narcotics Anonymous (NA): a Twelve Step program for drug addicts.

Nar-Anon: A Twelve Step program for family members of drug addicts.

Outpatient treatment: Two types. 1. Day treatment program is where an addict goes to the treatment facility all day and then goes home at night. 2. A less intense program where an addict works, lives at home, and goes to meetings several days or nights a week.

Over-reaction: a reaction that's not related to the actual seriousness or significance of the event or a reaction that normally would not trigger a similar response.

Sober living home or halfway house: A place where an addict stays after inpatient or outpatient treatment. The addict focuses on recovery and learning how to live sober by cooperatively living with other recovering addicts.

Sponsor: a sponsor is another Twelve Step group member who becomes a mentor. The sponsor and the sponsoree talk about the sponsoree's personal situations that come up, and the sponsor helps the member apply the program's Steps and principles to his or her life.

Stinkin' thinkin': a term used by Alcoholics Anonymous to describe the difficult personality characteristics that addicts often exhibit whether or not they are under the influence.

Substance Abuse: occurs when a person experiences adverse effects in one or more areas of life as a result of the substance use: legal, social, occupational, physical, material, or relational.

Substance Dependence: occurs when a person cannot stop using the substance, takes larger quantities than originally desired, continues to use despite known adverse effects, and experiences tolerance or withdrawal.

Tolerance: needing an increased amount of a substance to get the same effect. It's also the decreased effectiveness of the substance at the usual amount that occurs as the result of repeated use. It's the first sign of addiction.

Twelve-Step program: A program of recovery based on scriptural principles that include the idea that addicts and family members are powerless over their addiction, help from God is necessary to change oneself, confession of sins, the need to make amends, and the need to reach out to help others.

Walk on eggshells: Extra-cautious behavior so those around the addict don't upset him or her and set off an emotional deluge.

Withdrawal: Physical and psychological symptoms that result from the cessation or decrease of drugs or alcohol.

Working the program: involves continuing to apply the Twelve Steps and principles to one's life and working with a sponsor for accountability.

About the Author

KARLA DOWNING is a licensed marriage and family therapist, author, and founder of *ChangeMyRelationship.com*. Karla offers practical tools based on biblical truths to Christians in difficult relationships.

 NOTES

2

POST-ABORTION TRAUMA

Pat Layton

This chapter provides background information and leader resources for ministering to women who suffer physically, emotionally, and spiritually because they have had an abortion. Statistics reveal that after 30 years of legalized abortion in America, more than 40 million abortions have occurred.[1] This holocaust has resulted in not only the loss of innocent, unborn children, but also emotional, physical, psychological, and spiritual devastation of possibly a third of the women sitting in our churches today.[2]

These women feel captured by the silence of their shame. They wait for church leaders and ministers—their own leaders and ministers—to show them the path to God's healing, redemptive plan. We have the divine opportunity to offer these women hope, peace found in forgiveness, and ultimate freedom in Christ. We must help them surrender their secret, share their pain, and embrace the abundant life that only God provides.

Helping Women Heal from the Heartbreak of Abortion

Without question, abortion can be one of the most traumatic experiences women experience. Research suggests that more than 40 percent of women of child-bearing age have experienced the anguish of abortion.[3] Many women have been hiding their painful secret deep in their hearts; now they suffer severe consequences. They often wear smiles that hide their incredible burden.

Post-abortive women learn to live in silence and secrecy, stockpiling hurts and heartbreak they have buried deep inside. Many struggle for years with repressed memories, guilt, shame, and depression. Most post-abortion women feel they cannot talk about their abortion experiences because they made their "choice." They carry a great burden of shame and failure, afraid to reveal their hidden pain. Secrecy and shame are a destructive combination the post-abortive women are forced to endure in their self-imposed isolation.

As with any traumatic experience, many post-abortive women experience physical, emotional, and spiritual symptoms—all part of what is now called post-abortion trauma. These women may not even realize that their symptoms grow directly out of a past abortion.

Healing occurs best in the context of a redemptive community. As you provide an opportunity for women to join with a small group of other post-abortion women in a supportive and confidential environment, they share common experiences; out of this, healing and restoration can come. On the journey to healing, they will find a renewed sense of hope and purpose for the future.

Leadership Ideas

Establish a sense of openness within your church about the issue of abortion. Ask your pastor to address the subject of abortion from God's Word. Explain that as many as 43 percent of the women in the church may be harboring guilt and fear as a result of a prior abortion. Having his message accompanied by a five-minute testimony from a woman who has allowed God to heal her past will help open the door for other women in the church who need healing.

The Church—God's Voice

Every living person has been exposed to the effects of the 40 million abortions that have occurred in the United States since *Roe v. Wade*. The word *abortion* stirs a passionate debate both within the church and the community at large, in both pro-life and pro-choice circles. Everyone has an opinion.

Although the church has engaged to some degree in the moral and legal fight against abortion, it has sadly been virtually silent towards those who have been scarred by abortion. As a result, we live in a nation where both the government and many churches are being led by broken people. We, as the church, have an opportunity to help those hurt by abortion by offering the compassion, healing, and release that will allow these women to join God's army of truth.

Post-abortion trauma manifests itself through a variety of symptoms in men, women, grandparents, aunts, uncles, and siblings. These symptoms often lead to divorce, various kinds of abuse, and/or drug and alcohol addiction. The symptoms and their result in harmed lives provide a stronghold for the enemy—Satan. Someone once said that hurt people hurt people. When persons injured by abortion find forgiveness, healing, and wholeness, they break the cycle of hurting others as well as themselves. Families can be restored, marriages saved, and churches can be made whole again.

Society is filled with confusing messages for teens about sex and the value of life. They are bombarded with conflicting messages from the media, parents, other adults, peers, and pro-abortion rhetoric. They hear arguments about a woman's rights and freedom and men's failures and removal from leadership in the home. What better place is there than for the church to step up and proclaim truth? This is the time for the church to stand against the lie that abortion is an easy, available, and cheap alternative.

Without question, the laws need to change; but a greater place of power comes in healing in and through the church. Galatians 6:1 says: "You who are spiritual should restore [her] gently." It is the church's responsibility to provide a safe, healing environment in which restoration and reconciliation can occur.

Leadership Helps

1. Have literature readily available regarding post-abortion trauma in your church library or pastoral helps area.
2. Train pastors and church leaders about the "mission field" of women whose lives have been harmed by abortions.
3. Provide a post-abortion ministry contact in your information, website, and ministry services list.
4. Partner with your local crisis pregnancy center.
5. Offer post-abortion ministry and testimonies through your church's women's ministry events.

God's View/Biblical Perspective

O LORD, you have searched me and you know me. You know when I sit and when I rise; you perceive my thoughts from afar. You discern my going out and my lying down; you are familiar with all my ways. Before a word is on my tongue you know it completely, O LORD. You hem me in—behind and before; you have laid your hand upon me. Such knowledge is too wonderful for me, too lofty for me to attain. Where can I go from your Spirit? Where can I flee from your presence? If I go up to the

heavens, you are there; if I make my bed in the depths, you are there. If I rise on the wings of the dawn, if I settle on the far side of the sea, even there your hand will guide me, your right hand will hold me fast. If I say, "Surely the darkness will hide me and the light become night around me," even the darkness will not be dark to you; the night will shine like the day, for darkness is as light to you. For you created my inmost being; you knit me together in my mother's womb. I praise you because I am fearfully and wonderfully made; your works are wonderful, I know that full well. My frame was not hidden from you when I was made in the secret place. When I was woven together in the depths of the earth, your eyes saw my unformed body. All the days ordained for me were written in your book before one of them came to be. How precious to me are your thoughts, O God! How vast is the sum of them! Were I to count them, they would outnumber the grains of sand. When I awake, I am still with you. If only you would slay the wicked, O God! Away from me, you bloodthirsty men! They speak of you with evil intent; your adversaries misuse your name. Do I not hate those who hate you, O LORD, and abhor those who rise up against you? I have nothing but hatred for them; I count them my enemies. Search me, O God, and know my heart; test me and know my anxious thoughts. See if there is any offensive way in me, and lead me in the way everlasting.
Psalm 139

God creates all life. God sees all. God knows all.

Who Is She? A Picture of a Post-Abortive Woman

Can you spot someone who has had an abortion?

One third of women have had an abortion by the age of 45. This could be your neighbor, mother, sister, aunt, cousin, or daughter. Woman often easily say, "I wouldn't" or "I could never do that" … until they are confronted with an unplanned or unwanted pregnancy. Then their resolve can begin to crumble.[4]

Some women experience post-abortion trauma immediately; they process their feelings and move on. Other women exist in a lifelong state of denial and emotional confusion. Emotions can move from guilt to grief, from grief to regret, from regret to anger, and from anger to defensiveness.

A recent study reported that women experiencing the greatest degree of post-abortion trauma consider themselves pro-life or Christians. Some quote as many as 70 percent of women surveyed consider themselves "evangelical Christians." This same study reported 65 percent of post-abortive women experience multiple symptoms of post-abortion trauma. Women who choose abortion are married, single, young, and old. Abortion crosses all racial, social, and economic lines.

Common traits in women most likely to suffer post-abortion trauma include:
• have strong moral beliefs against abortion
• have conflicting maternal desires
• had the abortion during the second or third trimester
• felt pressured or coerced
• made their decision based on information that was inaccurate, biased, or inadequate
• are young in age or emotionally immature
• have prior emotional or psychiatric issues
• lack social support
• have had one or more prior abortions
• have experienced one or more prior miscarriages
• are less educated[5]

How Can We Help? Steps to Healing

The healing steps for post-abortion trauma are similar to those used in other forms of post-traumatic stress disorder (PTSD):
1. Share the story.
2. Look at the truth.
   • the world and abortion
   • the unborn child
   • God's role
3. Deal with anger.
4. Pursue forgiveness.
5. Work through grief.
6. Exchange bondage for freedom.
7. Conduct a release/memorial service.
8. Share the story so you can help others avoid making a tragic mistake or work through their own trauma.

Step 1: Share the Story

Each of us hides something we don't want others to know—possibly something about which we're ashamed. Satan knows that as long as he can keep us bound by our silence and secrets, as long as he can keep us isolated and separated from others, he can keep us from the healing and freedom God offers us.

Even before choosing to have an abortion, post-abortive women learned to live in silence and secrecy. They end up living with a stockpile of hurts that they have buried deep inside themselves. To free themselves from these hurts—not to mention avoiding the long-term emotional damage that repression can cause—they need to learn to recognize the lies they have accepted. These lies typically deal with their image of themselves, God, other people, and the world. Their false images keep them trapped in old wounds and unhealthy ways of living.

Today everyone hears myths and deceptions about sex, love, and life. Society has created a false culture of right and wrong. That's why Jesus spoke strongly about the deceiver, who plants so many lies in the world and in our hearts. Scripture reminds us:

> [The Devil] was a murderer from the beginning and has not stood in the truth, because there is no truth in him. When he tells a lie, he speaks from his own nature, because he is a liar and the father of liars.
> John 8:44

> Be sober! Be on the alert! Your adversary the Devil is prowling around like a roaring lion, looking for anyone he can devour.
> 1 Peter 5:8

One of Satan's goals is to isolate us and keep us ineffective as God's kingdom servants. Satan is the master deceiver. Deceit leads to the tendency to try to escape rather than face our wounds and pain. Unwilling to face intense emotions or take responsibility to go for help, post-abortive women let their burdens become their identities. They accept lies about themselves and God, and settle for living life in survival mode.

We all experience pain, and we choose different methods to try to escape it. Some of us ignore our problems with various—and tragic—coping mechanisms, such as drugs or alcohol. Others merely ignore their pain and then sink into depression. When tempted to depend on unwise or unsafe coping mechanisms, we must remember that the Enemy strategically shoots arrows or uses the wounds in our lives to distort our identities—our perception of who we are. If Satan can keep us feeling worthless, keep us feeling guilty, or keep our minds and hearts under his influence, he can keep us out of the glory in which we were intended to live—Have you read John 10:10 lately?—and out of the intimacy God wants to share with us. That's why the deceiver continually whispers lies about who we are, who God is, God's heart toward us, and the intimacy God wants us to share with Him.

Post-abortive women need to tell their stories to people they trust. This step has a purpose far beyond reopening old wounds. Sharing their experiences is the first step in the journey towards recovery, freedom, and healing. Healing almost always occurs best within the context of community or with a close prayer partner. God never intended us to struggle alone. We need each other; we were designed for strong relationships.

> Two are better than one because they have a good reward for their efforts. For if either falls, his companion can lift him up; but

pity the one who falls without another to life him up. Also, if two lie down together, they can keep warm; but how can one person alone keep warm? And if somebody overpowers one person, two can resist him. A cord of three strands is not easily broken.
Ecclesiastes 4:9-12

But a word of caution here: Advise post-abortive women to share their stories only with people they know they can trust!

Leadership Helps

1. Provide a safe environment where confidences are kept.
2. Give women opportunities to share their stories with trusted others who really listen.
3. Act as "truth mirrors" to help women see their true selves, not the masks they wear or their insecure, distorted beliefs about other people, God, and ourselves.
4. Offer acceptance without condemnation. (Jesus Himself said to a mob closing in to punish a woman caught in adultery, "Let him who is without sin cast the first stone.")
5. Encourage women to be there for one another, lending each other support, encouragement, and loving accountability.

> Make this your common practice: Confess your sins to each other and pray for each other so that you can live together whole and healed. The prayer of a person living right with God is something powerful to be reckoned with … My dear friends, if you know people who have wandered off from God's truth, don't write them off. Go after them. Get them back and you will have rescued precious lives from destruction and prevented an epidemic of wandering away from God.
> James 5:16,19-20, The Message

For a post-abortive woman, the thought of being "exposed" or "found out" is terrifying. Most likely, fear of exposure of the pregnancy motivated them to have an abortion in the first place. This may be the primary reason many women have guarded their secret for years. We must help women consider who they really protect by holding onto their secret. By covering up the lie that abortion doesn't hurt women, society's beliefs are reinforced that women are unaffected by the choice. Remaining silent keeps them in the darkness of the lie, but freedom comes in exposing it.

By offering a bold invitation to freedom and healing, we are breaking the power of secrecy that the Enemy has held women under for a long, long time. The healing journey process allows women to share with one another the secret of their darkest hour, a secret tucked away in their darkest places. This will be a giant step forward in developing trust among sisters in the group. God will use this time to change lives forever as women begin to trade a lie for the truth.

God's desire is not to expose our sisters, leaving them feeling alone and vulnerable. He's a protecting and caring Father who covers His children with grace, not shame. This process allows us to wrap our arms around hurting women and offer the protection of God as they expose their true Enemy.

Step 2: Confronting the Truth

For many women, the first emotion after having an abortion is immediate relief—relief that they're no longer burdened with an unplanned, unwanted pregnancy. Research indicates, however, that this relief is short-lived, soon replaced by guilt, shame, secrecy, sadness, and regret. This strong letdown experience is commonly referred to as post-abortion trauma. About 40 percent of post-abortive women experience traumatic responses to abortion; however, statistics reveal that 80 percent will experience some level of symptoms. Some psychologists believe the statistic actually may reach as high as 100 percent of women who suffer some measure of trauma.

Think carefully about these alarming statistics on the negative affects of abortion:
- 92 percent of post-abortion women experience emotional deadening
- 86 percent experience anger or rage
- 86 percent fear others will find out
- 82 percent experience intense feelings of loneliness or isolation
- 63 percent experience denial
- 58 percent battle nightmares
- 56 percent develop suicidal feelings
- 53 percent engage in drug abuse
- 39 percent have eating disorders[6]

They are everywhere—women and men who have bought the lie that abortion was their only choice, what they "had to do." The Alan Guttmacher Institute, a division of Planned Parenthood, estimates that 43 percent of American women will have an abortion by age 45. The institute also suggests that half of all pregnancies in the U.S. are unintended; out of those, 4 in 10 will end in abortion. In the U.S. alone, more than 1.5 million abortions are performed each year, making abortion one of the most common surgical procedures performed on women today.[7]

Why women get abortions:
- 75 percent said their baby would interfere with their lives
- 66 percent said they couldn't afford a child
- 50 percent didn't want to be a mother at the time
- 4 percent had a doctor who said their health would worsen with the baby
- 1 percent had a fetal abnormality
- 1 percent were victims of rape or incest[8]

Understanding the Truth About Life

Heated debate about when life begins still rages, but the Creator of life gives us a perspective about the lives of mothers and babies that can't be ignored.

> Oh yes, you shaped me first inside, then out; you formed me in my mother's womb. I thank you, High God—you're breathtaking! Body and soul, I am marvelously made! I worship in adoration—what a creation! You know me inside and out, you know every bone in my body; You know exactly how I was made, bit by bit, how I was sculpted from nothing into something. Like an open book, you watched me grow from conception to birth; all the stages of my life were spread out before you, the days of my life all prepared before I'd even lived one day.
> Psalm 139:13-16, The Message

We don't understand the amazing elements of creating a person's soul, but physical development alone is beyond what most of us would imagine:
- At 21 days the heart begins to beat.
- At 40 days brain waves can be detected by an electroencephalogram, commonly known as an EEG.
- At 6 to 7 weeks the baby can respond to touch.
- At 8 weeks he or she has every required body part.
- The duration of the pregnancy is for continuing growth of the fully developed body parts.

God knows what the unborn child is like in every cell of his or her body. He knows what the child would have looked like at 12 years old or as a young adult. Life does not begin with the first breath or the first heartbeat. Life begins in the heart and mind of God before conception. Women have been endowed with the incredible ability and opportunity to give life to eternal souls created in the image of God!

We have an amazing opportunity to assure women who have made tragic mistakes that Jesus knows where they are and He won't abandon them! Scripture assures us that God can and will forgive those who come to Him asking for His love and grace. We are unable to comprehend the extent of God's love, so why should we be deceived into thinking that God cannot forgive this sin?

Let's read some other portions of Psalm 139:

> Lord, You have searched me and known me. You know when I sit down and when I stand up; You understand my thoughts from far away. You observe my travels and my rest; You are aware of all my ways. Before a word is on my tongue, You know all about it, Lord. You have encircled me; You have placed Your hand on

me. This extraordinary knowledge is beyond me. It is lofty; I am unable to reach it. Where can I go to escape Your Spirit? Where can I flee from Your presence? If I go up to heaven, You are there; if I make my bed in Sheol, You are there. If I live at the eastern horizon or settle at the western limits, even there Your hand will lead me; Your right hand will hold on to me. If I say, "Surely the darkness will hide me, and the light around me will be night"— even the darkness is not dark to You. The night shines like the day; darkness and light are alike to You.
Psalm 139:1-12

The following checklist points to some of the emotions and behaviors exhibited by women who have suffered through one or more abortions. You can use this with women who might be considering joining your groups or to help women identify symptoms of post-abortion trauma.

- guilt
- drug abuse
- shame
- alcohol abuse
- depression
- anxiety
- unworthiness
- fear
- numbness of feelings
- deep regret
- thoughts of suicide
- reduced motivation
- excessive crying
- lack of trust
- abusive relationships
- promiscuity
- difficulty with intimacy
- difficulty sleeping
- appetite disturbances
- nightmares
- loss of interest in relationships
- acting out in rage and anger

God created us in His image (Gen 1:27). He also gave us the freedom of choice. Ever since Adam and Eve chose to disobey God, the world has been anything but paradise. Our freedom to choose has destroyed life across the ages.

But God willingly created us with the freedom to make our own decisions. We always have free choice, even though every choice always has consequences. Before entering the Promised Land, Moses challenged the Israelites, saying, "Today I have given you

the choice between life and death, between blessings and curses. Now I call on heaven and earth to witness the choice you make. Oh, that you would choose life, so that you and your descendants might live."
Deuteronomy 30:19, NLT

Step 3: Understanding Anger

God created our emotions—including anger—for our benefit. But when we don't express emotions properly, we can damage ourselves ... and others. The Bible says plenty about how to handle our emotions properly. Let's look at a verse in Ephesians that shows that anger isn't necessarily a sin.

> Since you put away lying, speak the truth, each one to his neighbor, because we are members of one another. Be angry and do not sin.
> Ephesians 4:25-26

"Be angry" in the Greek imperative tense is used for commands or direct instructions. Think about this: In this passage God actually commands us to be angry! Anger is almost always rooted in other emotions, such as fear, betrayal, injustice, and selfish ambition. Two key root emotions are (1) hurt or betrayal, and (2) frustration due to blockage of our goals. For example, we may feel our character was questioned or attacked, our rights were violated, our authority defied, or that something or someone we value was dishonored. These are only a few examples of how an underlying thought or feeling works its way through the "assembly line" of our mental factory and comes out as anger. Anger is a God-given emotion that helps us address issues, but it must be handled carefully. The goal must always be helping others, our relationships, and ourselves in the long run.

Two unhealthy ways of managing anger are (1) expressing it aggressively, and (2) keeping it all turned inside. Dr. Gary Chapman calls these methods explosive and implosive ways of handling anger. Implosive anger is internalized anger that is never expressed. "I'm not angry, just frustrated" or "I'm not mad, just disappointed" are common expressions of an imploder.

> Since you put away lying, speak the truth, each one to his neighbor, because we are members of one another. Be angry and do not sin. Don't let the sun go down on your anger, and don't give the Devil an opportunity. The thief must no longer steal. Instead, he must do honest work with his own hands, so that he has something to share with anyone in need. No foul language is to come from your mouth, but only what is good for building up someone in need, so that it gives grace to those who hear. And don't grieve God's Holy Spirit. You were sealed by Him for the day of redemption. All bitterness, anger and wrath, shouting and slander must be removed from you, along with all malice. And be kind and

compassionate to one another, forgiving one another, just as God
also forgave you in Christ.
Ephesians 4:25-32

Implosive anger can lead to passive-aggressive behavior, displaced anger, physiological and emotional stress, resentment, bitterness, and hatred. Imploders typically keep score, so the potential for a delayed explosion from a dormant volcano is always there. When Paul advised, "Do not let the sun go down on your anger," he was instructing us to deal with anger promptly and effectively before it spreads and does more damage. He also warned, "Do not give the devil an opportunity." Paul explains that poorly managed anger offers the devil a *topos*—a plot of land in our lives. He uses that *topos* as a military base from which to launch more attacks into our lives and relationships.

Explosive anger is the other unhealthy, ungodly management technique. It is characterized by uncontrolled fury that may come out as verbal and/or physical abuse. Explosive anger causes us to verbally attack by screaming, cursing, condemning, name-calling, humiliating, or threatening. It damages self-esteem and trust and ultimately destroys a relationship when the exploder causes the anger recipient to retreat for emotional safety.

Exploders frequently blame their victims for their anger or minimize their outbursts by calling them "blowing off steam" or "getting something off my chest." In extreme cases, the exploder may grab, push, or strike in anger. All unhealthy anger is harmful, but physical abuse is intolerable and protective measures should be sought. Don't try to justify or rationalize explosive anger—get rid of it and replace it with healthy approaches!

Don't sin by letting anger control you. Think about it overnight
and remain silent.
Psalm 4:4, NLT

Look after each other so that none of you fails to receive the
grace of God. Watch out that no poisonous root of bitterness
grows up to trouble you, corrupting many.
Hebrews 12:15, NLT

Unresolved anger finds unhealthy ways to express itself. Gary Chapman, author of *The Power of an Apology*, says,

"When one's sense of right is violated, that person will experience anger. He or she will feel wronged and resentful at the person (or persons) who have violated their trust. The wrongful act stands as a barrier between the two people and the relationship is fractured. They cannot, even if they desired, live as though the wrong had not been committed. Something inside the offended calls for justice." At the same time, he also acknowledges "something inside cries out for reconciliation."[9]

Post-abortive women often respond to experiences in ways they don't understand. They find themselves overreacting in ways they don't expect—sometimes with anger, other times with great sadness or hurt. As women begin their healing journey, they can begin to make sense of these uncomfortable emotions.

Anger Triggers in Post-Abortive Women
Review this list of situations and circumstances that might trigger anger in post-abortion women.
- baby showers
- pregnant women
- mothers with children
- hospital nurseries and birth events
- books about fetal development
- videos and television programs
- doctor visits for future pregnancy
- certain smells and odors
- specific sounds
- literature related to abortion
- pro-life/pro-choice advertisements and commercials
- other: _____

Anger Targets in Post-Abortive Women
As women come face-to-face with their abortion decision, they also may recall people who were involved in that choice. As they reflect on these people and their influence, these women often recall the confusion, pressure, and perhaps the feeling that she had no other choice. As a result, post-abortion women may aim their anger at many targets.
- people who withheld the truth about abortion
- the father of the baby
- friends who said abortion was the best choice
- parents
- themselves for allowing an unplanned pregnancy
- God
- doctors and nurses
- the abortion clinic
- extended family members
- the baby
- teachers or school counselors
- media
- church and religious leaders
- lawmakers
- other: _____

Often we hesitate to admit our anger toward others for fear of rejection. We find ourselves defending those we feel we should love. In order to heal, it's important to acknowledge anger and release it in a healthy way.

By opening God's Word to women, we help them see that God is big enough to handle even this. He will show each woman the way. Walk post-abortion women through the following checklist to help them deal with unresolved feelings.

Ephesians Anger Checklist
- *Assess your primary emotion*: Does your anger stem from loss of control, hurt, or indignation about wrongs?
- *Take off your mask*: Open up about what hurt you and talk through your feelings (Eph. 4:25-26).
- *Deal with issues and confront*: Communicate issues clearly and early. Be sure your goal is to resolve issues, not get back at people (Eph. 4:28). When dealing with issues face-to-face is not feasible, consider writing an "angry letter" you don't send. This often can be very healing.
- *Don't let anger fester and rot*: Unresolved anger is a written invitation to Satan to exploit us in wounding ourselves and others (Eph. 4:29).
- *God cares deeply about your anger*: Turn your anger over to God. His heart aches when we allow rage, resentment, or bitterness to take root and grow (Eph. 4:30).
- *Replace anger with forgiveness and compassion*: Because God has forgiven us in such a great way, we need to forgive others (Eph. 4:32).

Step 4: Forgiveness—God's Powerful Path to Freedom
Working through anger can be exhausting, but releasing anger lightens the load on the healing journey. The goal is to work through and begin to let go of anger, and to start moving toward forgiveness.

As you help women let go of anger, allow them to see their healing opportunities. Guide them to put the resentment they feel into God's hands. Holding on to anger and refusing to forgive are like drinking poison while waiting for someone else to die from its effects.

The next step is looking at the healing that comes not just from letting anger go but actually from forgiving our enemies. Encourage the post-abortion woman by telling her she is about to truly taste freedom.

We have allowed her to remember and respond to her abortion. She may find herself saying, "I want to stop being angry, but I just can't." Remind her—gently—that if she truly wants to experience healing, she will have to make a conscious decision at some point to let go of her anger.

In truth, God really wants her to go a step further: He wants her to forgive! In an area of our lives where we have been so hurt, it's difficult to imagine forgiving some of our offenders. But God can enable us to forgive! Take a moment here to help her understand what forgiveness is *not*.

Forgiveness Is Not ...

Forgiveness is not forgetting—We frequently hear the phrase "forgive and forget," but forgiveness does not imply amnesia. When God said He "will remember their sins no more," it doesn't mean that He suddenly has no recollection of an offense. It means that God does not catalog our sins and use the information against us.

Forgiveness is not minimizing the hurt—Forgiveness does not water down the offense by saying something like, "It's OK, it wasn't that bad," or "I know you didn't mean to hurt me." The truth is that a woman who has had an abortion because of the influence of someone else has been hurt deeply—perhaps even intentionally. Forgiveness does not say, *I'm all right; it's just a flesh wound*, when real trauma is involved. Instead, forgiveness calls the violation what it is in the same way an umpire calls balls and strikes in a baseball game.

Forgiveness does not necessarily mean reconciliation—Perhaps someone is thinking, *If I forgive the doctor, my ex-boyfriend, my parents, (whoever), then I have to initiate or at least be receptive to reconciliation.* Truthfully, some women are open to reconciliation and would give anything for that to happen; but reconciliation isn't even on the radar screen of some of the people involved in their abortion. The thought of a required reconciliation feels like being sentenced to life in prison without parole. Forgiveness recognizes that reconciliation may be neither possible nor wise following an abortion. Forgiving someone doesn't require becoming best friends ... or even close acquaintances.

God's View of Forgiveness

Consider some key passages about forgiveness.

> Since God chose you to be the holy people he loves, you must clothe yourselves with tenderhearted mercy, kindness, humility, gentleness, and patience. Make allowance for each other's faults, and forgive anyone who offends you. Remember, the Lord forgave you, so you must forgive others. Above all, clothe yourselves with love, which binds us all together in perfect harmony. And let the peace that comes from Christ rule in your hearts. For as
>
> members of one body you are called to live in peace. And always be thankful.
> Colossians 3:12-15, NLT

God commands forgiveness for our benefit. Forgiveness helps maintain harmony in relationships. It also creates deep peace and joy in the lives of the captives whom forgiveness sets free—your offender(s) and you!

A woman who has faced the pain and loneliness of abortion has the right to be angry with many people—at the very least the lawmakers, media, and medical community—people and agencies who are responsible for protecting life and ensuring that truth is communicated. Every woman has the right to be angry and to feel betrayed by some of her loved ones and her circumstances.

True forgiveness is seldom easy; in fact, forgiveness can be quite costly. But forgiveness is a powerful weapon for tearing down strongholds in our lives and hearts. The Enemy uses anger and refusing to forgive to keep us in bondage. When we surrender our unforgiving attitude and our anger, we set our own hearts free so God can take us to places we never dreamed possible.

It's common for post-abortion women to feel that, although God has forgiven them, they in turn need to forgive themselves. We must help these women understand that the Bible never identifies the need for us to forgive ourselves. The healing journey is designed to show them that the key is not forgiving themselves, but accepting God's forgiveness.

> For by grace you are saved through faith, and this is not from yourselves; it is God's gift—not from works, so that no one can boast.
> Ephesians 2:8-9

> He has rescued us from the domain of darkness and transferred us into the kingdom of the Son He loves, in whom we have redemption, the forgiveness of sins.
> Colossians 1:13-14

> We have redemption in [Jesus] through His blood, the forgiveness of our trespasses, according to the riches of His grace.
> Ephesians 1:7

> If we confess our sins, [God] is faithful and righteous to forgive us our sins and to cleanse us from all unrighteousness.
> 1 John 1:9

When Christians say, "I know God can forgive me, but I can't forgive myself," they are elevating their ability to forgive over God's ability. True healing and freedom only occur when the forgiveness God wants to give is accepted. In not completely accepting God's forgiveness, these women are essentially buying the lie that Christ's sacrifice on the cross was not sufficient to cover their abortion.

Step 5: Good Grief

By now we have helped the post-abortion woman begin the journey and move along toward forgiving those involved in her abortion. She is also beginning to understand and accept God's forgiveness. Now she needs to learn that the path of forgiveness is intertwined with the path of grieving. As her loss from abortion becomes more real to her, she will grieve more deeply and, in that grief, she will need to revisit the step of forgiveness. As she moves with your help to Step 5, she will focus on the importance of working through her grief.

Two Kinds of Sorrow

Any traumatic event in our lives will create sorrow. Many people who experience deep sorrow also can experience depression, turn to addictive behaviors, and allow a host of other dark influences on the soul to bring her down. The prophet Jeremiah found himself in a deep emotional pit, and shared his true feelings in that time. His words give us a picture of where destructive sorrow can lead:

> I gave up on life altogether. I've forgotten what the good life is like. I said to myself, "This is it. I'm finished. God is a lost cause." I'll never forget the trouble, the utter lostness, the taste of ashes, the poison I've swallowed. I remember it all—oh, how well I remember—the feeling of hitting the bottom.
> Lamentations 3:17-20, The Message

Grieving does not have to be destructive. God gave us the ability to grieve as a way to deal with life's difficulties and disappointments. The apostle Paul explains the difference between two kinds of sorrow in his second letter to the Corinthian church:

> Now I'm glad—not that you were upset, but that you were jarred into turning things around. You let the distress bring you to God, not drive you from him. The result was all gain, no loss. Distress that drives us to God … turns us around. It gets us back in the way of salvation. We never regret that kind of pain. But those who let distress drive them away from God are full of regrets, and end up on a deathbed of regrets. And now, isn't it wonderful all the ways in which this distress has goaded you closer to God? You're more alive, more concerned, more sensitive, more reverent, more human, more passionate, more responsible. Looked at from this angle, you've come out of this with purity of heart.
> 2 Corinthians 7:9-11, The Message

Previously, we looked at the importance of replacing lies—false beliefs that have been embraced—with truth from God. The women in your group need to allow their pain and sorrow to drive them towards God rather than away from Him. Only then will they experience transformation, healing, and new life.

Because past memories, sorrows, and hurts are uncomfortable, many women try to avoid them or find ways to escape the pain. And yet Paul was happy about the struggles and distress the Corinthians faced because these experiences spurred change. Jesus also promoted godly sorrow and gave those who hurt a wonderful promise.

The typical human response to many of the crises in our lives is to despise pain and endure or live with the shame. Unwilling to face intense emotions or take responsibility for our future, we let our burdens become our identity. Even some Christians accept lies about themselves and God and settle for survival rather than grasp the opportunity to move on toward real life.

Jesus refused to live in that shadow. He stayed in His pain, enduring the cross and shame that threatened to engulf Him, but did not let the pain and shame define who He was. We must experience our wounds and stay in our pain long enough to allow them to drive us to Jesus, then trust Him to help us find our way to victory and healing.

Looking hard at ourselves and our past hurts is very difficult. This would be frightening if we did not know that God walks with us side-by-side—indeed, He carries us. God cares deeply for every woman regardless of past experiences, and He longs for each of us to be free of denial and deception.

King David wrote Psalm 51 after his affair with Bathsheba. He had some serious baggage to handle with God!

> Be gracious to me, God, according to Your faithful love; according to Your abundant compassion, blot out my rebellion ... Surely You desire integrity in the inner self, and You teach me wisdom deep within. Purify me with hyssop, and I will be clean; wash me, and I will be whiter than snow. Let me hear joy and gladness; let the bones You have crushed rejoice. Turn Your face away from my sins and blot out all my guilt. God, create a clean heart for me and renew a steadfast spirit within me. ... Restore the joy of Your salvation to me, and give me a willing spirit.
> Psalm 51:1,6-10,12

The goal of remembering and the process of self-examination should entail seeking truth, making changes, restoring our relationship with God and others, and redemption.

As women truly share their feelings with God, He'll take these individuals along the path to healing. Most of us, though, have doubts about God's goodness and, specifically, about His heart toward us personally. Let's see what God says about us.

> Do not be afraid, for I have ransomed you. I have called you by name; you are mine. When you go through deep waters, I will be with you. When you go through rivers of difficulty, you will not drown. When you walk through the fire of oppression, you will not be burned up; the flames will not consume you. For I am the LORD, your God, the Holy One of Israel, your Savior.
> Isaiah 43:1-3, NLT

Fear is often the greatest enemy to meaningful life change. We long to return to what's familiar rather than take risks and face the unknown. More than anything else, the healing journey requires women to trust God. Healing the wounds in their innermost being will lead them along paths they never could have imagined. So, encourage them to take one day and one step at a time as they walk through life's shadows with Jesus, allowing Him to turn the shadows to light, to ease their pain, and then to lead them into freedom, truth, and the desires of their hearts.

Step 6: The Great Exchange—Bondage for Freedom

This step can help open minds and hearts to the incredible vistas that await post-abortion women at the summit of their climb toward wholeness and redemption. Each woman is more than she has become and more than she realizes even at this stage of forward movement. It's time to make the great exchange—to accept who she really is in Christ.

God's forgiveness, which comes with our confession, is a very powerful force. God's blessings don't stop when we receive salvation. He wants to help us really change. That happens through repentance. Unfortunately, "repentance" has been given a bad connotation over the years. "Repent" comes from the Greek word *metanoia*, which means to change *(meta)* our mindset or understanding *(noia)*. The word *metamorphosis* is a related term, meaning a change in form or substance, and is used to describe what occurs when a caterpillar emerges from its cocoon as a butterfly.

This change is a wondrous thing, but God does even more wondrous things for His children.

> "Pay attention, O Jacob, for you are my servant, O Israel. I, the LORD, made you, and I will not forget you. I have swept away your sins like a cloud. I have scattered your offenses like the morning mist. Oh, return to me, for I have paid the price to set you free." Sing, O heavens, for the LORD has done this wondrous thing. Shout for joy, O depths of the earth! Break into song, O mountains and forests and every tree! For the LORD has redeemed Jacob and is glorified in Israel.
> Isaiah 44:21-23, NLT

> Therefore, brothers, by the mercies of God, I urge you to present your bodies as a living sacrifice, holy and pleasing to God; this is your spiritual worship. Do not be conformed to this age, but be transformed by the renewing of your mind, so that you may discern what is the good, pleasing, and perfect will of God
> Romans 12:1-2

As we show women how to turn to God—giving Him their secrets, shame, false beliefs, and distorted perspectives—they become engaged in a battle of the mind and heart. Recall the model we discussed in Step 2, in which our wounds become infected with lies that lead to destructive agreements and a false sense of self.

We must realize that the battle for women's minds and hearts is an unseen battle, raging deep within each woman's innermost being. Their minds and hearts are not only the prize awaiting the victor in the battle but also are the battleground itself. God can and will transform every mind and heart given to Him. But each woman must turn to God in repentance and give her heart and mind to God. He will not turn us down, but neither will He force us to give ourselves to Him.

The risk of spiritual deception is high when we engage in battles for the minds and hearts of women. Satan is eager to attack us at our points of weakness. Too often Satan allows us to see ourselves only as the sum of all our failures. We get blinded to who we really are and how God sees us after we've placed our trust in Jesus to rescue and redeem us.

> Therefore, if anyone is in Christ, he is a new creation; old things have passed away, and look, new things have come. Everything is from God, who reconciled us to Himself through Christ and gave us the ministry of reconciliation
> 2 Corinthians 5:17-18

God has an adventure waiting for women as they begin to accept and appreciate who they really are and who He really is. Women who have given their lives to God become wise to Satan's scheme. Jesus brings amazing hope to all who hurt and feel they are being held captive. Jesus quoted Isaiah 61 to describe His mission in our world.

> The Spirit of the LORD God is on Me, because the LORD has anointed Me to bring good news to the poor. He has sent Me to heal the brokenhearted, to proclaim liberty to the captives and freedom to the prisoners; to proclaim the year of the LORD's favor, and the day of our God's vengeance; to comfort all who mourn, to provide for those who mourn in Zion; to give them a crown of beauty instead of ashes, festive oil instead of mourning, and splendid clothes instead of despair. And they will be called righteous trees, planted by the Lord to glorify Him. They will rebuild the ancient ruins; they will restore the former devastations; they will renew the ruined cities, the devastations of many generations … Because your shame was double, and they cried out, "Disgrace is their portion," therefore, they will possess double in their land, and eternal joy will be theirs.
> Isaiah 61:1-4,7

The Great Exchange

Paradise will come only when Jesus returns to take us into glory. He, too, longs for that day when He can be fully united with His people. But for now Jesus offers freedom from our captivity plus amazing gifts—we need only to embrace Him and the gifts He offers.

> I greatly rejoice in the LORD, I exult in my God; for He has clothed me with the garments of salvation and wrapped me in a robe of righteousness, as a groom wears a turban and as a bride adorns herself with her jewel.
> Isaiah 61:10

In healing process, we encourage women to pray Isaiah 61 with their names in place of such words as "me." It is also very effective to have a leader pray this Scripture aloud over the woman to whom the leader is ministering in order to allow her to truly hear and experience God's redemptive love.

Step 7: Release/Memorial Service

Eventually, the women meet together to do what their hearts have desired to do for a long time. The goal here is for the women to join their hearts, acknowledge their grief, and say goodbye to children they have lost. They are truly at a critical and special place in their healing journeys. This is the place where a woman can know that her wounds have been healed, her broken heart mended, and true reconciliation with her children accomplished. This is where God wants her to trade bondage for freedom, fear for courage, and shame for enduring joy.

This service becomes a time of closure, but also a time of remembrance and of new beginnings! Throughout the memorial service, we want to help women remember that they are God's children and are deeply loved by the Father. As women continue to grieve the loss of their children, they are free to mourn, to comfort one another, and to be comforted by others who have experienced the pain and have taken the journey they have been traveling.

Listen to God's plan for the future:

> Trust in the LORD with all your heart, and do not rely on your own understanding; think about Him in all your ways, and He will guide you on the right paths.
> Proverbs 3:5-6

> "For I know the plans I have for you"—this is the LORD's declaration—"plans for your welfare, not for disaster, to give you a future and a hope. You will call to Me and come and pray to Me, and I will listen to you. You will seek Me and find Me when you search for Me with all your heart."
> Jeremiah 29:11-13

Listen to what Jesus has done with past failures and sins.

> Yet He Himself bore our sicknesses, and He carried our pains;
> but we in turn regarded Him stricken, struck down by God,
> and afflicted. But He was pierced because of our transgressions,
> crushed because of our iniquities; punishment for our peace was
> on Him, and we are healed by His wounds.
> Isaiah 53:4-5

Consider what the Bible says about seeing her child again someday:

> David replied, "I fasted and wept while the child was alive, for I
> said, 'Perhaps the LORD will be gracious to me and let the child
> live.' But why should I fast when he is dead? Can I bring him back
> again? I will go to him one day, but he cannot return to me."
> 2 Samuel 12:22-23, NLT

> "Do not fear, for I am with you; I will bring your descendants
> from the east, and gather you from the west. I will say to the
> north: Give them up! and to the south: Do not hold them back!
> Bring My sons from far away, and My daughters from the ends
> of the earth—everyone called by My name and created for My
> glory. I have formed him; indeed, I have made him."
> Isaiah 43:5-7

Remember that we have settled many truths about what the Bible has to say
about life:
  • Not only is a child fully human from the moment of conception, but he or
    she has already been given a personal, eternal soul.
  • All prenatal existence is linked to a postnatal life. The life of our soul is an
    eternal spiritual continuum that begins at conception and continues into
    eternity.
  • God places infinite value on children from the moment of conception; each
    child is created and deeply loved by God.
  • At death, the unborn child immediately passes into the presence of God.
    Each of those little ones is present with the Father. They have identity and
    individuality; they deserve to be known for what they are: eternal beings.
  • As David looked forward to being reunited with his son, assure women in
    your group that a day will come when they will see their son or daughter in
    heaven. There we will live forever together.

Leadership Helps

During a time of prayer at the end of this session, encourage each woman to
"see" her child in her mind's eye with Jesus. Ask her to picture herself saying
goodbye to her child. Stand beside her, even hold her hand, as God leads her
to a moment of closure and peace. Many times a woman will hear or know her

child's name during this experience if she has not experienced it already. This becomes a bitter-sweet time of God's supernatural work in the lives of these women. He wants them healed, He wants them whole, He wants them to be free! He just allows us as leaders to play small parts in this amazing journey. This part of the healing journey does call for a spiritually mature leader who prays and eagerly strives to follow God in prayer. The *Surrendering the Secret Leader Guide* provides details and training for this prayer process.

Step 8: The Final Step to Healing—Share the Story Again!

As the women arrive at the summit in their healing journey, help them understand that completing the previous seven steps doesn't mean their journey has ended. This actually marks just the beginning. God not only has been present in the past of each woman who has experienced an abortion, He has been with them through this present journey and has a plan for their future!

> Your eyes saw me when I was formless; all my days were written in Your book and planned before a single one of them began.
> Psalm 139:16

> You've kept track of my every toss and turn through the sleepless nights, each tear entered in your ledger, each ache written in your book ... I'm proud to praise God, proud to praise God. Fearless now, I trust in God; what can mere mortals do to me? God, you did everything you promised, and I'm thanking you with all my heart. You pulled me from the brink of death, my feet from the cliff edge of doom. Now I stroll at leisure with God in the sunlit fields of life.
> Psalm 56:8,10-13, The Message

God is calling women to join Him in a great adventure. He has a unique role custom made for each woman. As they step outside of themselves to engage God's world and His plan for them, they also can acknowledge that completing the first pass through the seven steps doesn't mean there won't be additional emotional struggles as well as mountain-top experiences. Here's some of what God has in store for women who continue the journey with Him.

> "I [God] will repay you for the years that the swarming locust ate, the young locust, the destroying locust, and the devouring locust—My great army that I sent against you."
> Joel 2:25

> We speak God's hidden wisdom in a mystery, a wisdom God predestined before the ages for our glory ... But as it is written: "What eye did not see and ear did not hear, and what never entered the human mind—God prepared this for those who love Him."
> 1 Corinthians 2:7,9

God's provisions and promises for the future are incredibly bright! God has led women injured by the trauma of abortion along a path to healing; now He wants to use their stories and the truths they now understand to help other women who struggle with past decisions. Our goal now must be to discover and pursue God's purposes for their lives and to change their futures!

Revelation 12:11 shows the power of our stories by addressing the larger story and the coming final battle between good and evil:

> "They conquered him by the blood of the Lamb [Jesus] and by the word of their testimony, for they did not love their lives in the face of death."
> Revelation 12:11

There are three key truths to remember as the women pursue their role in the larger story.

Key 1: God wants them to live for something greater than themselves!

> For everything, absolutely everything, above and below, visible and invisible, rank after rank after rank of angels—everything got started in him and finds its purpose in him.
> Colossians 1:16, The Message

> I chose you before I formed you in the womb; I set you apart before you were born. I appointed you a prophet to the nations.
> Jeremiah 1:5

Key 2: They have been saved to serve God and healed to serve others!

> Don't be ashamed of the testimony about our Lord, or of me His prisoner. Instead, share in suffering for the gospel, relying on the power of God, who has saved us and called us with a holy calling, not according to our works, but according to His own purpose and grace, which was given to us in Christ Jesus before time began.
> 2 Timothy 1:8-9

> Do you not know that your body is a sanctuary of the Holy Spirit who is in you, whom you have from God? You are not your own, for you were bought at a price; therefore glorify God in your body.
> 1 Corinthians 6:19-20

Key 3: God's power is revealed in their weakness.

> Brothers, consider your calling: not many are wise from a human perspective, not many powerful, not many of noble birth. Instead, God has chosen the world's foolish things to shame the wise, and God has chosen the world's weak things to shame the strong. God has chosen the world's insignificant and despised things—the things viewed as nothing—so He might bring to nothing the things that are viewed as something, so that no one can boast in His presence. But from Him you are in Christ Jesus, who for us became wisdom from God, as well as righteousness, sanctification, and redemption.
> 1 Corinthians 1:26-30

As they learn to accept and appreciate who they are in Him and who He is in them, they will realize God has an adventure waiting for each of them.

To help women see themselves as God does, you can have each woman read Isaiah 61:1-3 aloud, replacing "me" with her name.

> The Spirit of the LORD God is on _____, because the LORD has anointed _____ to bring good news to the poor. He has sent _____ to heal the brokenhearted, to proclaim liberty to the captives and freedom to the prisoners; to proclaim the year of the LORD's favor, and the day of our God's vengeance; to comfort all who mourn, to provide for those who mourn in Zion; to give them a crown of beauty instead of ashes, festive oil instead of mourning, and splendid clothes instead of despair. And they will be called righteous trees, planted by the LORD to glorify Him.
> Isaiah 61:1-3

As you lead women to join with Jesus in His mission to bind up the brokenhearted, set captives free, and replace ashes with beauty, they will not believe how healing and powerful their past pain can be.

> Blessed be the God and Father of our Lord Jesus Christ, the Father of mercies and the God of all comfort. He comforts us in all our affliction, so that we may be able to comfort those who are in any kind of affliction, through the comfort we ourselves receive from God. For as the sufferings of Christ overflow to us, so our comfort overflows through Christ.
> 2 Corinthians 1:3-5

The amazing thing is that as we work with Jesus in setting captives free, we find that one of the captives becoming increasingly liberated from guilt and personal struggles is us—we who are the leaders! God has made some amazing promises to us if we are willing to raise our eyes above our current pain to Him and embrace the larger story. These promises give powerful incentive not to give up but to continue on to still more.

Women whose lives are bound by emotional and psychological chains that resulted from secret abortions are sitting in most of our churches, living as our neighbors, or even relating to us personally as our closest friends. Healed women sharing their stories could help set other women free. As Revelation 12:11 illustrates, unmatchable power lies within us as we take risks and become vulnerable by sharing our own experiences. At the very least, we can open our hearts and lives to them with a complete spirit of love, compassion, forgiveness, and the desire to help them become whole again.

At the same time, it's critical that we lead injured women to use wisdom and prayer to guide their sharing. God will show them how, when, where, and with whom He wants them to share. God would not have you injure or hurt others in the process of sharing. As leaders we have a wonderful opportunity to help healed women pursue ministry opportunities and partnership in women's ministry.

"She" who has been forgiven much loves much.

Leadership Helps

The post-abortion healing process found in *Surrendering the Secret* is an amazing journey used by God to set women free from the pain, heartbreak, and bondage of a past abortion. LifeWay women's resources are providing a variety of tools to equip church and ministry leaders to reach out to the "mission field" created by abortion. The Bible study *Surrendering the Secret* allows a woman to walk this journey alone or with a prayer partner. In an effort to assist ministry leaders in this new mission field, in-depth training is available through LifeWay Women's Training events. Advanced ministry training in the area of post-traumatic stress disorder will serve to provide more in-depth para-professional counseling ministry in many areas of crisis, such as divorce, abuse, addictions, loss of a loved one, and miscarriage.

The ideal setting for post-abortion ministry is in a small group led by a trained pastoral leader.

The vast numbers of women sitting in our churches today not only cry out silently for such ministry but are waiting to be used by God to reach others.

Recommended Reading
- *Secret Sin,* by Mary Comm, Morgan James, 2007
- *Surrendering the Secret,* Pat Layton, Serendipity House, 2007
- *Surrendering the Secret Leader Guide and Video,* Pat Layton, LifeWay, 2008

About the Author

PAT LAYTON is a wife, mom of three, and grandmother of five. She is founder and president of Life Impact Network, a Christ-centered parachurch ministry that includes crisis pregnancy intervention (A Woman's Place Ministries), an international post-abortion recovery program (Surrendering the Secret), a school-based teen abstinence program (Impact), and a Christian adoption agency (The Woven Basket) in Tampa, Florida. Since opening in 1986, the ministries have reached thousands of women, men, and teens in Tampa and across the nation. Pat is a national speaker and trainer for several organizations and ministries, including LifeWay, Heartbeat, and the National Council for Adoption. Pat writes a daily radio segment called "A Word for Women" and for several national organizations and publications. Her personal story has been published in a book called *Loved by Choice*. She is the author of a post-abortion healing Bible study called *Surrendering the Secret*, which is now available as an e-book.

Endnotes

1. National Right to Life, *http://www.nrlc.org/abortion/aboramt.html*.
2. Guttmacher Institute, *http://www.guttmacher.org/in-the-know/index.html*.
3. Ibid.
4. Ibid.
5. "Identifying High Risk Abortion Patients," David C. Reardon, PhD, *www.afterabortion.org*.
6. "Medical Report/Women's Health/Abortion ... Is there a Connection?" NOEL: noelinfor@noelforlife.org, accessed October 25, 2006. Abortion data from Reports of the Alan Guttmacher Institute: *www.religioustolerance.org/abo_fact3.htm*, accessed November 15, 2006.
7. Abortion data from Reports of the Alan Guttmacher Institute, *www.religioustolerance.org/abo_fact3.htm*, acccssed November 15, 2006.
8. "Medical Report/Women's Health/Abortion."
9. Gary Chapman, *The Other Side of Apology* (Moody Publishers, 1999).

Post-Abortion Self Assessment

Circle each answer.

1.	The abortion happened over a year ago.	Yes	No	Not sure
2.	I do not know the name of the doctor who performed it.	Yes	No	Not sure
3.	I was more than three months' pregnant when I aborted.	Yes	No	Not sure
4.	I was a teenager at the time of the abortion.	Yes	No	Not sure
5.	I was forced by others to abort.	Yes	No	Not sure
6.	The baby's father wanted me to abort.	Yes	No	Not sure
7.	The baby's father left the decision up to me.	Yes	No	Not sure
8.	Less than six people know about the abortion.	Yes	No	Not sure
9.	I always felt abortion was wrong, but had no choice in my situation.	Yes	No	Not sure
10.	I have experienced nightmares or flashbacks about the abortion.	Yes	No	Not sure
11.	Nightmares or flashbacks occur at least once each month.	Yes	No	Not sure
12.	There are details about the abortion that I cannot remember.	Yes	No	Not sure
13.	I avoid places, people, and things that remind me of the abortion.	Yes	No	Not sure
14.	I fear that my life may be short.	Yes	No	Not sure
15.	Since the abortion, I have lost interest in things I used to love.	Yes	No	Not sure
16.	I often have trouble sleeping.	Yes	No	Not sure
17.	I often feel angry and irritable.	Yes	No	Not sure
18.	Concentrating is often difficult.	Yes	No	Not sure
19.	I feel guilt and shame about the abortion.	Yes	No	Not sure
20.	I have cried over the abortion.	Yes	No	Not sure
21.	I use alcohol and/or drugs at least once per week.	Yes	No	Not sure
22.	I usually have sex with the men I date.	Yes	No	Not sure
23.	Sometimes I regret having the abortion.	Yes	No	Not sure
24.	I feel sad and depressed often.	Yes	No	Not sure
25.	I had physical problems after the abortion.	Yes	No	Not sure
26.	I feel bad emotionally at times for having had an abortion.	Yes	No	Not sure
27.	I feel that I made the right decision to abort.	Yes	No	Not sure
28.	I feel OK about the whole experience.	Yes	No	Not sure
29.	I would abort again to deal with an unplanned pregnancy.	Yes	No	Not sure
30.	I have had more than one abortion.	Yes	No	Not sure

Totals: ____ ____ ____

If the number of circles in your "yes" column exceeds 9, post-abortion trauma is probably affecting your life. If the number is higher than 14, you have numerous symptoms that need attention. If you answered, "yes" to 5 or more of questions 10-18, you may be struggling with post-traumatic stress disorder (PTSD) resulting from your abortion or some other trauma in your life.

Questions for a Leader to Help
with a Post-Abortion Discussion

1. How old were you when you had your first abortion?

2. What was your lifestyle at the time of your abortion?

3. Were you making poor choices in relationships with men?

4. What was your relationship with your parents?

5. Was there anyone in your life you felt you could trust completely?

6. What was your relationship with God?

7. How did you view abortion at the time (right, wrong, OK for some but not for me, etc.)?

8. When you discovered you were pregnant, what was your first thought?

9. Did you tell anyone about your pregnancy?

10. What emotions tended to overwhelm you as you thought about the pregnancy?

11. When did the idea of abortion first enter your mind? Was it suggested to you by someone?

12. Did you feel you "had no other choice" in the situation? What circumstances made you feel this way?

13. Did anyone offer support for the pregnancy?

14. How did you find the abortion facility?

15. Did you go alone or did someone take you to the abortion appointment?

16. When you first arrived at the clinic, how did you feel? (Some women report that they continued to hope that someone might rescue them.)

17. When you first entered the clinic, what did you see, hear, and feel?

18. What do you remember about the abortion procedure?

19. While you were recovering, what thoughts were playing in your mind?

20. Were there any complications with your procedure?

21. Who took you home?

22. What about you changed the day of the abortion?

NOTES

3

DOMESTIC VIOLENCE AND SPOUSE ABUSE

Karla Downing

This chapter seeks to provide background information and helps to assist those who minister to people experiencing domestic violence and spousal abuse. We will consider how God views these matters and present general legal issues and helps for assisting a woman living in an abusive or violent environment. As you seek to help, your purpose is to inform, support, encourage, and refer the woman who has placed her trust in you as a leader.

God's View

God does not condone abuse. Psalm 10 demonstrates clearly that He considers abhorrent any behavior used to control and hurt those who are weak.

> LORD, why do You stand so far away? Why do You hide in times of trouble? In arrogance the wicked relentlessly pursue the afflicted; let them be caught in the schemes they have devised. For the wicked one boasts about his own cravings; the one who is greedy curses and despises the LORD. In all his scheming, the wicked arrogantly thinks: "There is no accountability, since God does not exist." His ways are always secure; Your lofty judgments are beyond his sight; he scoffs at all his adversaries. He says to himself, "I will never be moved—from generation to generation without calamity." Cursing, deceit, and violence fill his mouth; trouble and malice are under his tongue. He waits in ambush near the villages; he kills the innocent in secret places; his eyes are on the lookout for the helpless. He lurks in secret like a lion in a thicket. He lurks in order to seize the afflicted. He seizes the afflicted and drags him in his net. He crouches and bends down; the helpless fall because of his strength. He says to himself, "God has forgotten; He hides His face and will never see." Rise up, LORD God! Lift up Your hand. Do not forget the afflicted. Why has the wicked despised God? He says to himself, "You will not demand an account." But You Yourself have seen trouble and grief, observing it in order to take the matter into Your hands. The helpless entrusts himself to You; You are a helper of the fatherless. Break the arm of the wicked and evil person; call his wickedness into account until nothing remains of it. The LORD is King forever and ever; the nations will perish from His land. LORD, You have heard the desire of the humble; You will strengthen their hearts. You will listen carefully, doing justice for the fatherless and the oppressed, so that men of the earth may terrify them no more.

On the other hand, certain Scripture passages are often cited to suggest that a woman should not defend herself or say anything to her husband about his mistreatment. A prime example is 1 Peter 3:1-6.

> "Wives, in the same way, submit yourselves to your own husbands so that, even if some disobey the Christian message, they may be won over without a message by the way their wives live, when they observe your pure, reverent lives. Your beauty should not consist of outward things like elaborate hairstyles and the wearing of gold ornaments or fine clothes; instead, it should consist of the hidden person of the heart with the imperishable quality of a gentle and quiet spirit, which is very valuable

in God's eyes. For in the past, the holy women who hoped in God also beautified themselves in this way, submitting to their own husbands, just as Sarah obeyed Abraham, calling him lord. You have become her children when you do good and aren't frightened by anything alarming."

These verses are often misused to support a warped concept of marriage. Submission was never intended to prevent a woman from having control over her own life and body.

A woman does not have to blindly obey her husband when he disobeys God's command to love his wife and treat her gently.

Paul gave God's command to husbands in Ephesians 5:25-29:

"Husbands, love your wives, just as also Christ loved the church and gave Himself for her, to make her holy, cleansing her in the washing of water by the word. He did this to present the church to Himself in splendor, without spot or wrinkle or any such thing, but holy and blameless. In the same way, husbands should love their wives as their own bodies. He who loves his wife loves himself. For no one ever hates his own flesh, but provides and cares for it, just as Christ does for the church."

A man does not love his wife as his own body if he is willing to destroy her life and the relationship. Abuse produces fear, but "God has not given us a spirit of fearfulness, but one of power, love, and sound judgment" (2 Timothy 1:7). God does not want a woman or her children to live in continual fear.

As Christians, we are to stand against evil and bring it into the light: "Don't participate in the fruitless works of darkness, but instead, expose them" (Ephesians 5:11).

For the good of the abuser, as well as the abused, abusers must be held accountable. Love has boundaries and is sometimes tough. God wants us to be aware of how people treat us. He has provided family, church, and government to help us protect ourselves from all types of abusive behavior.

Definitions

The following definitions can help victims to understand that what they are experiencing is not normal. Abuse includes any behavior that treats someone improperly, wrongly, insultingly, harshly, or injuriously. Abusive interactions tear down, disrespect, and devalue the relationship and the recipient. As a contrast, nonabusive relationships mutually respect, value, and empower the participants.

Spousal abuse can range from mild to severe and can intermittent to chronic. Many people react in a destructively in a moment of passion. However, if it is rare and acknowledged, it doesn't have the same effect as chronic abuse.

Types of Abuse

Several categories of abuse exist. They often occur together and are interrelated. Abuse can be verbal/emotional, physical, sexual, and/or spiritual.

Emotional and Verbal Abuse

This kind of abuse includes the following actions and behaviors. (This list is not meant to be exhaustive.)

- Nonverbal body language, including sneers, stares, and contemptuous looks and gestures that register disapproval, disdain, or threats.
- Blame for relationship problems, the abuser's actions, and events outside the marriage relationship.
- Manipulation, including the deliberate use of mind games and strategies to control or get one's way.
- Withholding affection, approval, money, information, resources, attention, and participation in the relationship.
- Name-calling.
- Denial, which can include lying about actions, motives, thoughts, events, and feelings. The abuser can also pretend not to remember when, in fact, he or she does.
- Threats about physical violence toward animals, children, spouse, spouse's relatives or friends. The abuser can also threaten to withhold any of the mentioned things or threaten to have an affair or take the children.
- Ordering the spouse to do things like a child, using an authoritative voice.
- Minimizing or making light of spouse's emotions, concerns, needs, thoughts, accomplishments, and interests.
- Intimidation through threats, looks, stares, sneers, use of an authoritative voice, and demands that the spouse do what is demanded "or else." It's an attempt to control or frighten the spouse.
- Yelling, raging, or expressing hostile anger.
- Interrogating or demanding an answer to questions the way the abuser requires and not tolerating the spouse to answer on his/her own.
- Humiliation in front of others through criticism, comments, punishment, or cruel jokes. This is purposeful degradation.
- Accusations including attributing feelings, motives, and intentions to the spouse and accusing him or her of doing things without proof.
- Devalue and disrespect involving put downs, undermining achievements, sarcasm, interrupting, harsh criticism, rudeness, belittling, and anything else that communicates contempt and disregard.
- Ridicule, including mocking, telling jokes, belittling remarks, insults, and making fun of efforts and individuality.
- Ignoring spouse's requests and needs, purposefully not responding to conversation, and silent treatments.

Physical Abuse

Physical abuse does not occur alone; it is always accompanied by verbal and emotional abuse. Physical abuse includes using physical actions to threaten harm or do actual harm.

Although they differ in their ability to injure, physical abuse can involve hitting, beating, slapping, pushing, shoving, pulling hair, or pinching. It also includes unwanted physical restraint, including holding someone down or locking a person in a room.

The abuse can involve ripping clothes, threatening violence with a weapon, or using verbal threats or innuendoes about future violence.

Physical abuse can include holding up a fist or appearing to be ready to strike, destroying property, throwing objects, and hurting pets.

Sexual Abuse

Sexual abuse is defined as using intimidation or force to coerce a spouse into unwanted sexual acts. The abuser believes that the spouse has no right to say no and forces this belief on his/her spouse.

Spousal rape is forcing a spouse to have sex against his or her will. You can check your state's laws with your local police department or women's shelter. Most states have laws that make spousal rape illegal.

Sexual abuse includes:
- Demanding sex after an abusive incident.
- Threats and manipulation to pressure a spouse into uncomfortable sexual acts.
- Threats if the spouse says no to sex.
- Ridiculing a spouse's sexual performance.
- Comparing a spouse's body or sexuality to others.
- Using sex as a bargaining tool or withholding to punish.
- Shaming masculinity or femininity with inappropriate comments or insults.

Spiritual Abuse

Spiritual abuse is the misuse of spiritual authority and power. Scripture is often used to manipulate, intimidate, control, or criticize the spouse.

The husband can misuse his authority as the head of the family to demand servant-like obedience. God has made the husband the "head of the wife" (Ephesians 5:23). However, this "master of the house" mentality elevates the man's own needs and feelings and disregards his wife's needs and feelings. It can be used to justify making decisions without her input and controlling her. By demanding she submit, the abusive husband can silence her, refuse to listen to her, and get his way.

Demanding submission, while ignoring the mandate that he is to love his wife "as also Christ loved the church and gave Himself for her" is spiritual abuse (Ephesians 5:25). Colossians 3:19 says, "Husbands, love your wives and don't become bitter against them." Men who misuse their spiritual authority do it in a way that devalues their wives; their actions are abusive.

The man can also misuse his authority to mistreat his children by demanding obedience and making himself above questioning. It is an arrogant attitude of "I am the head of this house. You will do what I say and shut your mouth. God put me in charge of you and you better obey me or else." This harsh authoritarian attitude is obviously abusive to the children but also abusive to a wife. It's painful for her to see her children mistreated and be powerless to do anything about it. Colossians 3:21 says, "Fathers, do not exasperate your children, so they won't become discouraged."

This father may be more concerned with how decisions affect himself than his family. He may believe he owns the children, and they are there to serve his needs. It is common for an abusive man to use the children to punish his wife, induce guilt in her, threaten her, manipulate her, or control her. He can do this by punishing or interacting with the child in a way that hurts his wife. She may come to fear his mistreatment of the child and do what he wants to prevent it.

Child Abuse

Ephesians 6:1-3 tells children to respect and obey their parents:

> "Children, obey your parents in the Lord, because this is right. Honor your father and mother—which is the first commandment with a promise—that it may go well with you and that you may have a long life in the land."

Verse 4, however, warns parents, especially fathers:

> "Fathers, don't stir up anger in your children, but bring them up in the training and instruction of the Lord."

Parents can stir up anger in their children through abuse.

Children are more likely to be abused physically, sexually, and verbally/emotionally in homes where abuse in the parental relationship occurs. Observing abuse toward another family member is called "vicarious abuse." Studies show it causes the same problems as actually being abused. The child feels helpless, responsible, guilty, and fearful, often believing it is his or her fault that the parent or sibling is being abused. Abused children have problems in school, low self-esteem, physical and somatic complaints, loneliness, depression, withdrawal, problems with peers, hyperactivity, poor impulse control, and an increase in anti-social behavior, acting out, and aggression. They are also at an increased risk of being abused or abusive in later relationships.

Many states consider it a form of child abuse when the child observes physical abuse in the home. In extreme cases, Child Protective Services may remove the child from the home.

Gender Differences

Both men and women act abusively in relationships. Women, being more verbal than men, can attack, retaliate, and tear down their husbands with words. Both use abusive tactics in response to difficult marriage dynamics such as substance abuse, workaholism, dysfunction, addictions, affairs, or spousal abuse in an effort to force change or resolve problems.

Many couples report incidents of mutual mild physical abuse, often occurring during an argument, which may involve restraint, throwing objects, slapping, pushing, grabbing, or shoving. Although this level of violence is harmful to the marital relationship and should be avoided, it often occurs out of momentary frustration and is not likely to escalate. However, when a spouse who is also verbally and emotionally abusive uses violence, it has more significance and may be a sign that the abuse is increasing.

Battering involves beating, choking, sexual assault, and use of weapons that result in serious injury. Severe battering involves a pattern of control, escalates over time, and usually involves more serious injury. Ninety-seven percent of battery is committed by males (Johnson, Michael P. & Ferraro, Kathleen J., "Research on Domestic Violence in the 1990s: Making Distinctions," *Journal of Marriage and the Family*, 62, November 2000, 948–963).

What does all this mean to you? If the woman to whom you are ministering admits to hitting her husband or throwing something at him, take the context into consideration. She may be acting out of frustration or self-defense. Don't let this deter you from believing that she could be in an abusive relationship. Help her see that responding this way is ineffective, risky to her, harmful to the children and her marriage, and increases the risk of her husband becoming increasingly physically abusive in retaliation. Encourage her to think of alternative ways to respond, such as leaving the room or house and refusing to argue.

A woman in an abusive relationship needs to understand the implications if she resorts to violence even out of frustration or retaliation. Her abusive husband may purposely provoke her into hitting him and then report her to the authorities to gain an advantage over her in the legal system and to threaten her with losing the kids in a future custody battle. State domestic violence laws usually do not take the context into consideration and often do not understand abusive relationship patterns and what would provoke a woman into hitting her husband. Women can be prosecuted for responding physically to an abuser's verbal and emotional abuse, removed from the home, and subsequently have a distinct disadvantage in further legal matters.

The Chronically Abusive Relationship

All abuse devalues, disrespects, and tears down the partner's individuality and personhood; however, chronic abuse is based on power, control, and manipulation.

Power is the need to feel superior. The relationship is perceived as a power struggle with the spouse as a threat rather than a partner. The abuser undermines the partner's attempts to work together or cooperate and convinces their spouse that he/she has no rights to change the situation.

Control is always an element of an abusive relationship. Some abusers control everything, but most control specific areas. It may show up as jealousy and possessiveness by managing the spouse's activities and time, possibly even forbidding him or her to leave the home.

Control of money is also common. The abuser may take the spouse's paycheck, withhold funds, require a strict accounting of all money spent, refuse to give adequate money for needs, or make the spouse beg for money.

Control could also be exercised over decisions. Taking away or withholding items to punish is also common. Manipulation is accomplished through direct and indirect methods to get the abuser's way and to undermine the spouse to keep him or her off balance and dependent, doubting himself or herself so the abuser can keep the power in the relationship.

Hostility—rather than good will—permeates the abusive relationship. Good will is manifested by caring, kindness, empathy, and a concern for the spouse's well being, as well as the relationship. Hostility is a sense of anger, contempt, negativity, and disregard for the spouse's well being and the relationship. Since the abuser does not value the spouse's feelings or the health of the relationship, the abuser will not care about the effects of the abuse.

Before we examine portraits of the chronically abusive man and woman, let's consider a question that you might hear later.

Can the abuser change? Yes, but it usually takes direct interventions, lengthy therapy, and the realization that they will lose their wife and children if they don't. Change involves an understanding of what is abusive, a willingness to take full responsibility for the abuse, getting outside help, not blaming the abuse on anyone or anything else, and a sincere desire to change. A man will have to change the underlying beliefs he holds about himself, his wife, and the relationship. As long as he holds the entitlement view where he is supposed to be treated a certain way and believes that he should have the power and control in the relationship, he will resort to abusive behavior; he will feel justified. He needs to develop respect and empathy for his wife and give her the space and time she needs to heal and feel safe with him. If he pushes her, she will see it as a sign that he has not changed, because he cannot accept her feelings. Abusive men can be charming and manipulative and can convince people to believe they are changing when they really are not.

A Portrait of the Chronically Abusive Man

Men are more likely than women to engage in abuse based on power, control, and manipulation. Most of the literature written on abuse focuses on men who abuse women. Since you are dealing with spousal abuse toward women, the rest of this chapter will focus on the abused wife.

If you know the husband of the woman claiming to be abused, it may be difficult for you to believe that this man can do the things she is telling you. He may be successful, respected in his job and outside relationships, spiritual, normal looking, and nice with positive characteristics. This does not mean she is not telling you the truth. Many abusers are competent in other areas of their lives and have a dual personality. Even with their wives, the husband can be gentle, kind, and loving when they are not being abusive. Abuse crosses all socioeconomic levels, nationalities, and occupations.

The abuser does not accept blame for any problems in the relationship and will rarely admit fault. If he feels guilt for how he treats her, he will say she makes him do it or he can't help himself. He may even blame it on his job, outside circumstances, mistreatment in prior relationships by other women, or his childhood. He will also blame her for circumstances in his life. If he has a problem on the job, it's her fault. If the children do something wrong, he blames her. He may even blame her for being upset with him when he treats her abusively, telling her she is too sensitive, always complaining, nagging, or pushing to get her way.

When she points out an incident of abuse to him, he may focus on how it is upsetting him for her to bring up the problem or focus on the fact that she yelled back at him, ignoring the names he called her to start with. He may deny or excuse it, accuse her of lying and making it up, or accuse her of provoking him.

Ironically the man may even accuse his wife of being abusive to him. However, his definition of abuse is quite different than hers. He calls it abusive when she gets angry with him when he mistreats her and when she defends herself. He also thinks it's abusive when she tries to tell him he can't treat her in this manner or when she tries to get him to listen to her.

An abusive man knows what he is doing when he is abusive. The only exception to this is a mental illness, which is rare. Abusers don't just lose control; they plan to use abuse and can control what they do. They can monitor how far they go during a physically abusive incident to insure they hit in places that cannot be seen and can stop themselves from doing what they consider unacceptable or wrong. Even if intoxicated from drugs or alcohol, the abuser knows what he is doing. Substance abuse does not make a man abusive, but it can contribute to more severe abuse and a lowering of his inhibitions, resulting in more abusive episodes with greater violence.

An abusive man may be extremely possessive, wanting his wife to be there exclusively for him. He may even be jealous of the time she spends with their children. He may seek to undermine any outside relationships she develops, including treating her friends and relatives offensively so they won't come around. Unreasonable jealousy results in suspiciousness, making it difficult for her to have any interactions with other men without being accused of having an affair or wanting to. This can even result in following her, looking through her things, listening in on phone conversations, and other monitoring activities designed to prove she is unfaithful. It is also possible that she will be punished or abused based on these accusations. Ironically, it is the abuser who is likely to be unfaithful, not his wife, even while he is accusing her.

The abuser changes rules. One day it is OK to fix food a certain way. The next day he may throw it away, telling her she is a rotten cook. She tries harder to please him, trying to figure out what she did wrong. The fact is she didn't do anything wrong; he changed the standard so that he had an excuse to be displeased with her.

The abuse usually intensifies when the wife appears to be getting independent, detached, or doesn't react to the abuse like she used to. If the abuse isn't working, he has to intensify it to maintain control or lose the power he has over her.

Abuse is learned. Most abusive men come from homes where they were abused or observed abuse. When a man sees his father abusing his mother, he learns that he is supposed to treat women that way. When he is abused as a child, he learns that love involves control and hurting others, so he continues to use that pattern of behavior as an adult.

A Portrait of the Chronically Abused Woman

Regardless of the type of abuse, a woman is generally affected the same way. She feels the abuse is her fault and that it will stop if she can just get "it" right. Feelings range from confusion, anxiety, and depression to fear, panic, and loneliness. She doubts herself and develops a low self-esteem. When her husband denies the abuse and minimizes her concerns, she spends a significant amount of time trying to figure out what really happened, replaying their interactions over and over, attempting to reconcile his account with hers.

Her tendency is to minimize the severity of the abuse and its effects on her. She may get to the point that she's so used to it she doesn't even realize it is abuse.

Abuse is cyclical with distinct phases. This was first identified by Lenore Walker in her book *The Battered Woman* (HarperPerennial: New York, New York, 1979, pg. 55-70). The first phase is called the tension-building stage where small abuses occur increasingly, but the woman ignores their significance and accepts that they are her fault, while the abuser denies doing anything.

These small abuses build up to an acute battering incident, which will become a major event and escalate the abuse. If physical abuse is used, it may involve injury. If the abuse is verbal and emotional, it will escalate the intensity, throwing her off balance, getting her attention because it is impossible to ignore.

After the escalation, the kindness and contrite loving behavior begins where the abuser will be nice and caring. He may appear to show remorse by apologies, gifts, and promises. This may be the only time she gets treated well in the relationship. She is relieved, wanting to believe and hope he will stay this way; but something inside her knows he will not.

A woman is most likely to reach out for help during the acute battering phase, because the shock that "it" happened again brings despair, hopelessness, and desperation. Then when things calm down, she may doubt herself, thinking her reaction was overboard, and feel relieved that it really isn't as bad as she let herself believe. She may then feel ashamed that she told you about the abuse.

An abused woman will try to reason with her abuser in getting him to see that she is not doing, saying, or thinking what he is accusing her of. She tries to resolve conflicts with him by explaining what she meant, not realizing that he does not want to reach mutual understanding since his goal is control and power over her. She may try to tell him how his abuse hurts her, thinking that when she finally explains it in a way that he understands, he will stop. She doesn't realize that he knows it hurts and wants to do it anyway. Rather than seeing her as conciliatory, he views her attempts to explain and reach an understanding as her way of trying to overpower him.

She spends a significant amount of emotional and mental energy trying to please him so he won't get upset at her. She is always aware of his ever-changing moods and catches undertones in his body language and speech. At times, he is a nice guy and may seem reasonable or even contrite and wounded, desperately needing her. At other times, he is belligerent and angry, capable of being mean and cold toward her. She believes that she did something wrong to change him into this mean man and if she can figure out what it is, he'll be nice again. So she keeps trying.

Unproductive arguments and conversations happen frequently. The abusive husband does not want to talk about what really happened or listen to his wife's concerns. He may change the subject to divert or mislead or use any other abusive tactics to avoid healthy resolution. He might even say that it's a wrong time to bring up any conflict since they're getting along so good at that moment. She's left feeling confused and hopeless.

The intense confusion she feels comes from the difference between her reality and his. Since she believes he cares about her and doesn't understand that he is willingly hurting her, she gives value and weight to his perceptions and feels confused when they differ from hers. The more this happens, the more she doubts herself.

During an encounter, she may feel like she's crazy. "What really happened?" she asks herself. "I thought I was being nice, but he just accused me of being mean. Was I mean? I don't think so, but maybe I could have said it a little softer or not brought up two things at once. Maybe I should have realized that he was in a bad mood from work and waited to ask him. I never get things right. I'm so stupid."

Her words and actions are often twisted and misconstrued. He may interpret her offer to help him as accusing him of being weak. A comment regarding his harsh discipline of a child will be interpreted as her trying to tell him what to do and telling him he is a failure as a father. Her request to find out what is bothering him may be misconstrued as her being nosey and pushy. She may be told that her attempts to cook a nice meal for him are manipulative. Her explanations defending herself may elicit accusations of her being right all the time, arrogant, and always wanting things her way.

This woman may be too embarrassed to tell people what is happening. She may have tried and may not have been believed, since the abuser may have a good reputation with outsiders. Most abusers do so in private and try to present a different public image. Since verbal and emotional abuse is insidious and baffling, she may have difficulty explaining why it is so bad and why she feels the way she feels. The conversations and interactions she is having may not sound that bad on the surface. Yet the impact comes from the motives of the abuser, the double messages, and the confusion and devaluing of his partner—all difficult to convey.

Leave or Stay?

Leaving an abusive relationship is difficult because the woman believes many of the things her abuser says. As long as she doubts herself and minimizes the abuse, she will stay. The abuser knows this and seeks to keep her off balance and undermines any independence or strength she gains. He also tries to keep her isolated from other people and from getting help so she won't leave. Plans to leave could bring anger, remorse, promises to change, more abuse, or an attempt to ruin her reputation. He may threaten her life, threaten to take the children, threaten to leave her penniless, threaten to kill himself, or threaten to "make her pay" if she leaves. Most women leave and return multiple times before they finally leave for good or require change.

It is important not to tell a physically abusive man that his wife is leaving because it may escalate the violence. The risk of major violence increases for a time when the woman first leaves. Risks include violence toward herself, her children, a new boyfriend, or anyone else close to her. It includes sexual assault, stalking, accusations, threats, intimidation, and possibly murder.

In situations where she leaves a severely physically abusive husband, she may need to inform others of the danger, consider a restraining order, or contact the police. This woman may have to vary the routes she drives for regular activities, tell family and friends not to give her information to him, and not contact her husband herself. Some women have had to take on a new identity and leave their old life behind completely.

Abusive men rarely agree to a separation to work on the relationship. Fearing her independence, an abusive man doesn't want to give his wife a chance to see how life is without him. He also doesn't accept her right to dictate the terms of their relationship because he doesn't want to give her equality or power in the relationship.

You cannot know for sure which men will be violent, but the following signs are correlated with the increased possibility of violence:

- Her intuitive sense of what he is capable of doing. Women usually know.
- Prior extreme violence, possessiveness, and jealousy.
- Prior serious violence with weapons or threats to use weapons or kill.
- Violence during a pregnancy.
- Use of prior terror tactics like hurting animals or stalking.
- Substance abuse.
- Escalation of threats and violence.
- Prior sexual violence.
- Serious depression with no hope for the future.
- His plan and fantasy about suicide or homicide.

So Why Does She Stay?

One of the most frustrating things about dealing with abused women is that they stay in their situation and continue to tolerate the treatment they're receiving. One of the most common reasons is financial. Even those who have adequate resources do not want to change their financial status and lifestyle. Others will truly be destitute if they leave.

Society and pressure from her church are additional factors to "keep the family together." She is afraid of what he will do if she leaves, afraid to be alone, and afraid of divorce. She feels guilty and blames herself for the problems. She still hopes things will get better. She believes his threats about her leaving. She believes she cannot make it without him. If she saw abuse or was abused as a child, she accepts it as normal. She knows she will have to deal with him anyway after the separation or divorce, so she reasons it is easier to stay.

You cannot make her see the situation. Getting a clear understanding of the abusive relationship dynamics takes time. Unless there is change, gaining enough strength to leave also takes time. In the meantime, you can be there to support and strengthen her.

It is not your role or responsibility to fix her or help her sort out the complex dynamics in her marriage. When you recognize the signs of spousal abuse, listen, support, and refer her to sources that can help her.

Also watch for physical signs of personal destruction. This woman might start using drugs, alcohol, or prescription drugs to cope. She might either deprive herself of proper nutrition or do the opposite and use food to help soothe her hurt. She may feel depressed, with feelings of hopelessness and helplessness. Although some physical symptoms are real, often physical complaints and illnesses such as headaches, stomachaches, body aches, weakness, fatigue, depression, anxiety, insomnia, nervousness, lack of concentration, and others are psychosomatic.

Legal Issues

In the case of physical abuse, she may need to seek protection in the form of a restraining order. There are three types: An Emergency Protective Order is obtainable from a police department and is usually good for five business or seven calendar days. The woman has to show she is in immediate danger as evidenced by a recent abusive incident or serious threat. It is served to the abuser.

A temporary restraining order lasts for approximately three weeks and is granted by a judge in cases where there is physical abuse, a serious threat of emotional or physical abuse, sexual assault, or stalking. The abuser is notified in advance of the hearing.

A permanent restraining order is issued by a judge after a hearing and lasts for three years. It may say "no contact" or "no violent contact." In extreme cases, the restraining order is permanent. No Contact Orders are issued by the juvenile court ordering the abuser not to have contact with minor children, if they are in danger.

A woman should keep the restraining order with her at all times because an officer would need to see it before he can do anything about a violation.

Restraining orders do not insure a woman's safety or insure that the abuser will not harass, contact, or harm her. In fact, the threat of physical abuse increases when a woman files a restraining order. This needs to be taken into consideration when the decision is made to file, as she may need to make arrangements to stay safe. Laws differ in various states regarding the penalties for violation of a restraining order. You can check with your local police department or women's shelter for your state's specific laws.

Domestic violence is a crime. In response to the huge number of women who refuse to prosecute and testify against their abusers after they are arrested, some states have passed laws that allow the district attorney to pursue the case without the woman's testimony. Sentencing can include probation, a batterer's treatment program, fines, counseling, substance abuse treatment, a suspended sentence with probation, and jail time for repeat offenders. Abused women are sometimes ordered to attend a personal empowerment program.

Counseling

Your purpose is to inform, support, encourage, and refer.
- Help her to understand abuse, focus on how she is being affected, and recognize that she has choices.
- Help this woman to see that the things her husband is telling her are not true. He may be telling her she is mean, a bad mother, stupid, or a bad wife. Help her to look at the proof that those things are not true. Read together several Scripture passages that remind her of God's unconditional love. Some of these include:

> Genesis 29:31-35: God saw Leah's pain from not being loved by Jacob and blessed her with children.

> Psalm 17: David's prayer for justice

> Psalm 37: a contrast between the wicked and the righteous

> Romans 5:1-8: We have peace with God through Jesus despite trials.

> Romans 8:28-39: We are more than conquerors through Jesus.

- Help her to understand that God's heart hurts when He sees abuse. Reassure her that God is not punishing her for past mistakes.
- Do not be shocked or put down this woman with statements such as, "I would never put up with that! Why are you?" You don't know what you would do in the same situation. She may have said the same thing.
- If she comes to you during an abusive incident and later minimizes it because things seem better, explain to her that this cyclical pattern is further evidence of an abusive relationship and that it will happen again.
- This woman needs validation. She may recite incidents and ask you, "Is what he did right? Did I say the wrong thing? Would you feel that way?" She needs to hear that it is not right for her husband to treat her that way, regardless of what she does. She needs to hear you call it "abuse."

- If you tell her to look at her part in the abusive relationship, you are saying the same thing as her abuser–that it is her fault.
- Don't tell her to submit to her abusive husband or to love him. These ignore the realities of her situation and make her feel that the abuse is her fault. Telling her to submit undermines her need to take care of herself and her right to refuse to be treated abusively.
- Help her to understand that no matter what she does, the abuser is responsible for his behavior. She does not cause him to be abusive. It comes from within him and is his choice. You can agree with her that she is like all of us: she is not perfect, will make mistakes, and may even react wrongly at times. However, nothing she does justifies his abuse. That is a separate issue.
- Agreeing with her that it is better to keep the father in the home is agreeing that she should accept the abuse and that the children are better off with an abusive father than without one. This is one of the excuses she uses to stay.
- Believe her. Don't question her perceptions.
- Treat her with respect and reaffirm that is how she should be treated.
- Don't tell her what to do. Let her have control of her own life. Don't tell her she has to leave or stay.
- Reminding this woman that she needs to stay true to her marriage vows or reminding her that she cannot divorce for abuse is telling her she has to stay in the situation and undermining her need to see the abuse as serious.
- Help her to see that it is impossible to please her husband and do everything right. His abusive attitudes and beliefs set her up to fail.
- Help her to see she cannot explain herself to him. He won't let it work.
- Help her to understand that control does not equal love and a man who loves her will value her and treat her with respect.
- Recognize signs of physical abuse: long sleeves in summer, absences from regularly scheduled meetings, and excuses for frequent bruises and injuries.
- Pray with her and for her.
- Offer help for physical needs.
- Don't confront the abuser or tell him what she told you. He may retaliate.
- Keep her disclosures confidential.
- Encourage her to keep a journal of the abusive behavior.
- In the case of physical abuse, help her to develop a safety plan. Tell her to keep an emergency escape kit in her car or at a friend's house that includes clothes, money, important papers, and other essentials. Refer her to a shelter. Give her the National Domestic Violence Hotline number: 1-800-799-SAFE (7233). Research local facilities, if available, and have phone numbers, websites, and addresses available.
- Refer her to professional counseling, recommending therapists who know how to handle abuse situations. Encourage her to go alone to the counseling session.
- Recommend materials.
- Give her a Bible if she does not already own one. Mark Scriptures for her to read to encourage her.

- Help her to know that divorce is not a reflection of her worth and that she will still be accepted and supported by the church. Remember that God hates divorce, but He does not hate the divorced person.
- If she tells you about physical, sexual, or severe emotional child abuse, you may be required under law as a mandated reporter in your state to report the abuse to Child Protective Services. To check your state's laws, call Child Protective Services or your local police department.
- Be patient. It is difficult to leave an abusive relationship. Don't judge your success or failure with her by whether or not she leaves. Tell her that it takes time to get strong enough to see the situation clearly. She needs to make the decision fully on her own; otherwise, she's just obeying yet another person in her life who's telling her what to do—even if it is good advice.

Recommended Resources

10 Lifesaving Principles for Women in Difficult Marriages, Karla Downing, Beacon Hill Press of Kansas City, 2003.

Angry Men and the Women Who Love Them: Breaking the Cycle of Physical and Emotional Abuse, Paul Hegstrom, Beacon Hill Press of Kansas City, 1999 and revised 2004.

The next two resources are not Christian, but are helpful in the area of domestic violence and abuse.

The Verbally Abusive Relationship: How to Recognize It and How to Respond, Patricia Evans, Bob Adams, Inc. Publishers, 1992.

Why Does He Do That?: Inside the Minds of Angry and Controlling Men, Lundy Bancroft, G. P. Putnam's Sons, 2002.

National Coalition Against Domestic Violence website: *www.ncadv.org* or call their National Domestic Violence Hotline at 1-800-799-SAFE. Get additional information and/or find local women's shelters.

About the Author

KARLA DOWNING is a licensed marriage and family therapist and the author of *10 Lifesaving Principles for Women in Difficult Marriages, When Love Hurts: 10 Principles to Transform Difficult Relationships,* and *The Truth in the Mirror.* She is also the founder of *ChangeMyRelationship.com.* Karla offers practical tools based on biblical truths to Christians in difficult relationships. She also has a passion to teach ministry leaders how to minister more effectively to people in difficult relationships.

 NOTES

4

DEPRESSION

Barney Self, EdD

This chapter attempts to provide a greater understand-ing about the struggle called depression. The hope is that both those who struggle with depression and the people who assist them in the struggle will be able to address this issue better and in a God-honoring way. In the caregiving process you need to inform, support, assist, and potentially refer the woman in your church who has come to trust you as a resource.

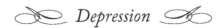

An Overview

Comfort the hurting and discover how serious the situation is.

When a woman comes to you and is tearful, upset, and overwhelmed with life and the trauma she is experiencing, try to comfort her and ask some key questions to help her deal with this reality. The questions are an attempt to clarify the symptoms listed later in this chapter.

Don't run to worst cases or fail to take the situation seriously.

Better to exhibit a serious, unwarranted level of concern than to fail to care appropriately for someone who is truly overwhelmed. This balance will become more discernable as you work with this person over time and see her patterns more clearly.

Don't panic. Present healing as a process.

Do not join this woman in her place of panic. If you do, she will likely be even more overwhelmed. The key is to understand that she did not get in this situation overnight and she will likely not be able to move from it immediately either. Remember that God is faithful and neither abandon her in her situation nor you as you seek to help her. Christ comforts us with the perspective that "My grace is sufficient for you, for power is perfected in weakness" (2 Corinthians 12:9). God is our strength, and we need to focus on giving to others what we have already received in His love, grace, peace, comfort, and hope.

In the same mentality, healing is a process that will likely take time. The duration is based on the severity of the struggle and the individual's partnership healing. God certainly still performs miracles, but we are also subject to the view that Paul puts forth in Philippians 1:6, "He who started a good work in you will carry it on to completion until the day of Christ Jesus." Understand and help her come to a place of acceptance of God's timing and the pattern of recovery as a process.

Call the struggle what it is—depression.

While working in close proximity with the women you serve, you may see signs of trauma, pain, or sadness for which they simply fail to account. It may be up to you as their leader to help them understand the severity of what they are facing and what kind of impact it either has or may have on their lives. If the symptoms are clearly defined (based on the list in this chapter), clarify for them that depression is likely what they are facing.

Overcome Denial

Denial may be a powerful response to your suggestion that this woman is dealing with depression. She may have a stigma attached to such a malady and might develop a pattern of anger or a rejection of your future assistance based on this mindset. Be willing to stay connected and to continue to love and reach out to her.

Responses that might soften the situation:
- I could be wrong (about your depression), but some symptoms of depression seem to be present in a powerful way in your life."
- "I hope you are right (about not being depressed), but my fear is that life will simply get worse and your relationships will suffer if you are wrong. Can you really run that risk?"
- "I don't want you to hurt because I care very much for you and want your life to be the best it can be. Please check this out with your doctor and let her or him make that call."

Define the Illness

Depression has an impact on literally every aspect of a person's life. It is an illness that involves the individual's body, emotions, thoughts, behavior, and interpersonal relationships. Technically it's referred to as a mood disorder which means that a person's mood takes on the prevailing feelings of sadness or despair.

Depression is one of the most prevalent struggles women face today. The inherent life stressors generate depression with great frequency. Women tend to experience depression about twice as frequently as men. Women in ministry roles within the church will be confronted consistently with this struggle either in their own lives or in the lives of those to whom they offer care and counsel—or both. Many women will be unaware that they are dealing with this serious issue. Consequently, knowing the warning signs that signal depression can assist the caregiver in helping the individual minimize the trauma in recovery from those symptoms.

Symptoms of Depression

Depressed mood for most of the day, for more days than not, either by their own account or observed by others.

While depressed, presence of two or more of the following:
- poor appetite or overeating
- insomnia or sleeping much more than normal
- low energy or fatigue
- low self-esteem
- poor concentration or difficulty making decisions
- feelings of hopelessness, helplessness and guilt
- inability to enjoy normally pleasurable activities or interests including sex
- significant weight change (+ or – 5 percent of body weight in one month)
- feelings of restlessness or lethargy
- recurrent thoughts of death or suicide
- persistent physical symptoms that are unresponsive to treatment such as headaches, chronic pain, or digestive disorders

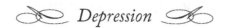

(Adapted from the American Psychiatric Association: Diagnostic and Statistical Manual of Mental Disorders, Fourth Edition, Text Revision. Washington, DC, American Psychiatric Association, 2000.)

Depression can create a struggle for the individual to maintain normal relationships with those people who are important in her life—family, friends, coworkers. The individual's work attendance, work performance, and work relationships may suffer as the depression takes its toll. Pivotal roles such as wife and mother may also suffer because of the struggle to cope with the ongoing depression. Self-esteem will be diminished when depression causes her performance to be less than she or others might expect. Ultimately, to be depressed is to suffer.

Causes of Depression

Depression can be generated by a variety of causes. In general, depression is fostered by losses: physical, emotional, relational, or otherwise.

Some people are born with a genetic pattern from their family of origin that would make them more susceptible to depression than others. Others have no family history of depression but are affected by the illness anyway.

One of the factors that can create depression is changes in an individual's body. Often depression occurs after the birth of a baby. Menopause can also trigger the onset of a depressive episode. Other changes in the body or physical losses including cancer, infertility, major surgery, or other medical conditions can generate depression.

Grief brought on by a loss can also be a major trigger for depression. Losses can include loss of job or dream, divorce, death of a loved one, or even retirement.

Stress brought on by life's relentless pressures can also generate depression over time. Sometimes the alignment of several factors simultaneously overwhelms the individual. Consider dealing with a difficult marriage relationship, a job status change (positive or negative), a child's struggle in school, and a parent's illness at the same time. Any one of these might be handled with little problem but collectively they may overwhelm the person's ability to cope and continue to function without becoming depressed.

Gender Differences

Women tend to handle depression differently from men.
Women tend to:
- turn inward
- blame themselves for being depressed
- have difficulty staying in control
- strive to be nice
- pull away when hurt
- try to fix things by trying harder

- self-medicate with food, friends, and a focus on emotional needs
- feel guilty about the depression
- procrastinate
- exaggerate weaknesses
- disintegrate when failure is the outcome
- try to think through the depression
- have increased appetites and weight gain

Men, on the other hand, tend to:
- blame others for the depression
- act out their inner turmoil
- strive to maintain control at all costs
- be overly hostile and irritable
- attack when feeling hurt
- try to fix the depression by problem solving
- turn to sports, TV, sex, or similar activities
- feel ashamed by the depression
- become compulsive
- be terrified of their own weakness
- strive to maintain a strong male image
- try to act away the depression ("I'm not depressed.")
- turn to alcohol and other substances

(Adapted from *Unmasking Male Depression*, Archibald D. Hart. Word Publishing, 2001.)

The list for men is included in this study because the women who come to you for assistance may be doing so because their husband is depressed and they are feeling overwhelmed and incapable of handling his struggle.

Is Depression a Sin?

The answer is absolutely "No!"

We can do things in God's permissive will that cause pain and suffering for ourselves. However, even the sadness that follows such mistakes is not sin. Take David and Bathsheba for example. Their child died and they were overwhelmed. Was sin involved? Absolutely! Was their depression sin? No. Even though it was generated by a sinful act, their depression was a normal reaction to a major loss. You can read more of this story in 2 Samuel 11–12.

Depression is the body's natural response to the stressors and losses of life. If a person is experiencing clinical depression, the issue has gone far beyond a spiritual or emotional problem. Chemical imbalances in the brain are as debilitating as a heart attack. While we would rush a person with heart trauma to the doctor, many well-meaning Christians advise against medical care for the depressed person.

We struggle in body, mind, and spirit to reconcile the pain that life generates. We read in the Old Testament that Elijah defeated the prophets of Baal and shortly thereafter had this perspective: "I have had enough! LORD, take my life" (1 Kings 19:4). He was overwhelmed after having encountered massive amounts of stress in representing the nation of Israel in calling down fire from heaven. It was not a spiritual issue for Elijah or the fire would have not come down. He would have been standing before the crazy prophets of Baal with wet wood. It was, however, a stress-and-depletion issue. You can read more of this story in 1 Kings 18:1—19:18.

Another Scripture passage that shows God's response to sadness and depression is Jesus' encounter with Mary and Martha after Lazarus' death. Jesus knew why Lazarus had not come when he had been summoned. He understood that raising Lazarus from the dead was to be the crowning miracle of His ministry—outside of His own resurrection—and that after Lazarus arose they would have a party to end all parties. Even so, when Mary approached Him tearfully the shortest verse in the Bible proclaims, "Jesus wept" (John 11:35). Jesus' honesty with His own feelings challenges us to be honest and straightforward in dealing with our own. It also challenges us to be gentle with others in their times of sadness and to be willing to join them in that pain as Jesus did. He was the ultimate compassionate caregiver.

When we are overwhelmed, we need to do exactly what Christ did in His overwhelmed moments of Gethsemane—"My Father! If it is possible, let this cup pass from Me," (Matthew 26:39)—and the cross—"My God, My God, why have You forsaken Me?" (Matthew 27:46). Jesus kept His face turned intently toward God. We must do the same. Claim the position we read in Romans 8:1, "No condemnation now exists for those who are in Christ Jesus." We must refuse to allow shame to enter into the picture. Satan is the great accuser and loves to try to debilitate us with false guilt. Keeping our eyes on Jesus allows us to avoid this trap.

Staying connected to God and accepting His grace and forgiveness in our brokenness is what allows us to move beyond the stuck places that depression creates in our experience. We must truly allow God to be God and view ourselves in the same way that He views us: as His perfect children (Romans 8:1) who are broken ("I do not do the good that I want to do, but I practice the evil that I do not want to do," Romans 7:19). We are His awesome children who struggle. We must be very careful to be compassionate to others in their pain and to avoid being judgmental. If we do judge, we pretend to be God, and that is sin.

Staying connected to God means continuing to study the Bible and pray for His healing and hope. It also challenges us to see the traumas that life generates from a different perspective. As Christians we must view life through the lens of Romans 8:28: "We know all things work together for the good of those who love God: those who are called according to His purpose." God wants to bless us through every crummy, miserable, worthless, hurtful, and painful thing that life throws our way.

The perfect example of the nature of God is the life of Christ. In the midst of His ultimate trauma—receiving your sin and all of the rest of the sins of the world—God brought about the greatest blessing the world has ever seen: Christ's resurrection and our salvation! That is God's nature and why we can offer Him to those who are hurting. You don't know how He will make things better, but you do know that God's nature is unchanging. If He allowed something to occur, He will bless us through it if we partner with Him in it.

Our job as spiritual guides for the depressed is to help people hold on to the truth about the nature of God without condemning them for their actions or feelings. If a clear-cut sin issue exists, we can agree that they sinned and challenge them to repent while at the same time we can love them as people and have compassion for them in their pain. We must love the sinner and hate the sin because that mirrors God's stance toward us: He loves us and hates our sin.

Depression generates some very warped thinking processes. Our view of ourselves, of each other, of life, and of God is skewed. We must take every thought captive (2 Corinthians 10:5). That means we must challenge every conclusion and thought about life that we have. Returning to the truth that is God's view is critical in moving forward and defeating the pattern that depression puts in place.

Treatment

Relationship is a powerful healing tool—trust is the key.

The power you have to make a difference in another woman's life cannot be overstated. You have the power to generate encouragement, healing, hope, and change. For this pattern to occur, a place of safety must be built so that this individual understands that she can trust you not to be judgmental, condemning, or negative. Instead, she needs you to be affirming, supportive, and a window into God's view of her own life as well as her feelings. The trust built is in direct proportion to opportunity for change and healing to occur.

What if your best efforts to provide care still do not produce a pattern of recovery? What are the other options for depression treatment?

Medical treatment can provide needed relief for depression.

Encourage your counselee to seek the assistance of her primary care physician. If she does not have one, ask if she has a gynecologist. This doctor may be able to refer her to a primary care physician. If she has no physician relationships, offer several options of physicians in your church or whom you know and trust from your own experience. In any case, she needs to see a doctor as soon as possible. Depression can affect many of the body's functions, and a good check-up would be beneficial to understand what bodily systems might have been affected. A good diagnostic evaluation will include a history of symptoms, their severity, whether they are reoccurring, and a history of treatment. In addition, a physician will likely ask about a family history of depression and a history of the treatment they received.

The Basics of Physical Health

As self-evident as they may be, good nutrition, physical exercise, appropriate rest, and the use of a multivitamin supplement are essential elements in generating recovery from depression. They empower an individual and give them tangible things to do to make a difference in their quality of life and the recovery process. Verify that these elements are included in the counselee's life and daily pattern so that recovery can be maintained.

Medication can be a tremendous ally in overcoming depression.

Many Christians believe that depression can be overcome by simply praying and reading the Bible more. While this is always a powerful and positive part of life, it may have little effect on the depression. This is not a spiritual issue! Instead, it is a chemical imbalance issue. The chemical out of balance is serotonin. Serotonin is produced by the base of the brain (medulla) and on a good day is utilized by the frontal lobe (cerebral cortex), the part of the brain with which we think.

When David wrote, "This is the day the LORD has made; let us rejoice and be glad in it," he was having a good serotonin day (Psalm 118:24). After Elijah called down fire from heaven you read his perspective a few verses later and it is like, "I have had enough! LORD, take my life" (1 Kings 19:4). This was a really bad serotonin moment for Elijah.

Stress causes the frontal lobe to stop using serotonin. The base of the brain that produces it simply reabsorbs it when it gets the message that it was not used. This is similar to cooking for the family, calling them to dinner, and no one coming. The efficient thing to do is to put the food in the refrigerator. Basically, that is what the base of the brain does with the serotonin; it reabsorbs it. Anti-depressant medications block that process, forcing the frontal lobe to use the body's natural answer for depression—its own serotonin. This is the only thing the medication does. It continues to force the use of the serotonin on the think-ing part of the brain, allowing the body to heal itself. Even if the medication is used long-term, it is still God-honoring. It honors God because the serotonin helps us to respond to our feelings rather than react to them. It allows us to hold on more accurately to the truth of what we know about God and life. It allows us to see life more realistically and live out our faith more accurately. It allows us to generate the abundant life that God so much wants for us.

Christian counseling/therapy offer a powerful healing option.

Therapists have been trained in treating depression and its inherent effects. Christian therapists will also offer a spiritual connection in the healing process. It is in the therapeutic and spiritual alliance that the therapist, counselee, and God form the healing triangle. You can be an ally to the therapist in fostering change and healing. (Information on making a referral is found in the Introduction).

Research suggests recovery from depression occurs most effectively with a combination of therapy and medicine.

Neither is as effective as both are in tandem. This is true because medication will often facilitate the individual's ability to confront her struggle and deal with the feelings it generates more directly. Often we can encourage those who are willing to see a therapist to consider the option of medication with their physician. We can also encourage those who are open to medication to seek the assistance of a therapist to assist in facilitating change and relief from the symptoms of depression.

Spiritual struggles can be part of the struggle with depression.

Sometimes well-meaning people can create a heightened sense of guilt and shame because the person is experiencing depression. Bildad, Zophar, and Eliphaz had best intentions to help their friend, but were by Job's own account "miserable comforters" (Job 16:2b). We need to avoid that position and we also need to help those struggling with depression to deal with the theological misunderstandings that may be present from whatever the source. Engage the pastor or other trusted spiritual leader to partner with the counselee and with you to dispel those theological demons that continue to haunt God's beloved.

Embrace God's love and reject the shame and guilt.

All the sources of intervention need to be focused on creating a pattern of health and restoration in all of life's relationships, especially with God. By being the hands and voice of a loving Father to this one, His daughter, you can truly be God's instrument of healing and truth. You can help her to remember the truth that God is love. In addition, He has known her from before the beginning of time and, if she is a believer, has chosen her to be His daughter. She is desperately loved by God who was willing to offer His Son as a sacrifice just for her.

If this woman has guilt about unrepented sin, then the sin issues need to be dealt directly with God who has promised to forgive us and cleanse us from all unrighteousness (1 John 1:9). Guilt from God regarding His laws and requirements as His children is good because it helps us to recognize that we need to make things right in our relationship with Him and to change our behavior.

False guilt, on the other hand, is bad because it is tied to others' judgments and perspectives, not God's. False guilt is someone else's attempt to manipulate us into doing what they would prefer. It is nothing more than their opinion. We have options of whether or not we would choose to follow their direction.
Shame is our recollection of our faults, flaws, mistakes, and problems. Satan loves to use this to condemn us and cause us to be focused on ourselves and our struggle. God would have us to keep our gaze on Him, on His forgiveness, and on our restoration.

How to Help Yourself If You Are Depressed

Depression can make you feel exhausted, worthless, and hopeless. It can create a cloud of negative thinking and lethargy. This quagmire can be overcome in the treatment process, but here are some options to pursue in the meantime:

- Set reasonable and attainable goals and be reasonable about the amount of commitments you make.
- Set priorities and break tasks into reasonable segments that make them more workable.
- Seek out those people whom you can trust, depend on, and be real with.
- Do activities that boost your morale.
- Get out of the house. Go to a movie, a ball game, or certainly to church. Do social activities that may give you a positive experience.
- Don't expect miracles in the treatment process. Be patient with yourself, medicine (if applicable), and therapy. Getting over depression takes time.
- Don't make major decisions during this time. Postpone them until you can think more clearly and deal with the feelings more honestly. Include others whom you trust in the decision-making process.
- Replace negative thinking with positive thinking. This is a choice. Give yourself time to make the transition.
- Allow your family and friends to assist you in facing this struggle.

Depression Assessment Instrument

Circle the response that most closely matches your feelings over the past few weeks:

(1) *Never/Rarely*   (2) *Sometimes*   (3) *Most of the time*

1. I have been feeling blue, sad, unhappy, or down in the dumps.
       1   2   3

2. I have been feeling tired and fatigued.
       1   2   3

3. I have been feeling hopeless.
       1   2   3

4. I have been feeling irritable, uneasy or restless.
       1   2   3

5. I have gained or lost significant weight over the past two months.
       1   2   3

6. I have difficulty sleeping or want to sleep too much.
       1   2   3

7. I have difficulty enjoying pleasurable activities.
       1   2   3

8. I have lost interest in sex or have sexual difficulties.
       1   2   3

9. I have difficulty concentrating or making decisions.
       1   2   3

10. I have been feeling inadequate or like a failure.
       1   2   3

11. I have been feeling tremendous guilt without reason.
       1   2   3

12. I have experienced crying spells.
       1   2   3

13. I have had recurring thoughts of suicide or death.
       1   2   3

TOTAL _____

*This instrument is for discussion purposes
and is not intended to provide a definitive assessment.*

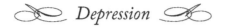

Notes on Depression Assessment Form
- Pay special attention to the items that are marked with a two or three.
- Twos may be threes in reality. Ask questions about the person's perspective regarding the term "sometimes." How often is that the case?
- The threes are red flags that need to be attended to carefully and understood clearly.

About the Author

BARNEY SELF is a licensed marriage and family therapist who has practiced for the past 30 years in the Nashville area. He received his master of religious education and doctor of education degrees from New Orleans Baptist Theological Seminary with a focus in psychology and counseling. Dr. Self served as LeaderCare counselor for LifeWay Christian Resources from 1999 to 2007. In that role he answered over 4,300 phone calls from the ministry body of the SBC. Dr. Self has become well acquainted with ministry life and its inherent pressures. In 2008 he joined the staff of Forest Hills Baptist Church as pastoral counseling minister. He and his wife have been married for 39 years and have two grown children and six wonderful grandchildren.

NOTES

5

PRODIGAL CHILDREN

Vicki Arruda and Chris Adams

This chapter seeks to provide background information and helps to assist those who minister to persons with a prodigal child. We will take a look at each character in the situation and the roles they might play. We also will provide five principles to help you minister to the parents. Within each principle, you'll read the struggle of a mother with a prodigal child. As you seek to help, your purpose is to inform, support, encourage, and refer the woman who has placed her trust in you as a leader.

The Characters

The Prodigal Child

Webster's Dictionary defines the word "prodigal" as "recklessly extravagant; characterized by wasteful expenditure; one who spends or gives lavishly and foolishly." A prodigal child is reckless regarding consequences their living brings on themselves, family, friends, and others. A prodigal is one who has turned away his or her heart from home and the Lord.

The Parents

Prodigal children don't come from a prototype family. We're mistaken to believe that prodigal children come only from homes with major parent-child conflicts, divorce, abuse, blended families, or religious abuse. While homes with these dynamics are certainly more conducive to producing a prodigal child, prodigals also come from healthy and strong Christian homes. We also can't rule out the effects of genetic make up, temperament, spiritual gifts, birth order, and sin nature, which can contribute to the behavior of a prodigal as well.

Siblings

Siblings in a home with a prodigal can develop resentment toward him or her or the parents because so much focus and energy is given to the prodigal. Sometimes the siblings resent both the prodigal and the parents. They feel they are cheated of their parent's attention and affection. Parents often overcompensate for the prodigal's behavior and become too hard on their other children, fearing that they will become prodigals. Often so much emotional and physical strength are spent on the prodigal that little is left for other family members.

Extended Family and Friends

These two resources can be very helpful to the parents of prodigal children. Unfortunately, they can also be very harmful. Whether family and friends help or harm is often determined by whether they have had a similar struggle and how they handled it.

Hearing from others with similar life experiences is very helpful for parents of prodigal children, even if the results have been less than ideal. Another parent living in faith and hope can give struggling parents courage to walk in faith, trusting God with their child.

Unfortunately, wounded people wound people. If family members and friends are early in their journey with their prodigal child, they may not be helpful.

Additionally, many friends and family members may not understand or agree with how a parent deals with a prodigal child. Sometimes showing tough love to protect the child at risk is the most difficult decision a parent makes.

The Church

Often the church is the last place families reach out to for help. We as leaders need to develop resources to help members cope with various family dynamics, such as a prodigal child. One such resource is a referral list. See the Introduction for more information on how to make a referral.

God's Word is clear that we will all face trials.

> "Consider it a great joy, my brothers, whenever you experience various trials, knowing that the testing of your faith produces endurance. But endurance must do its complete work, so that you may be mature and complete, lacking nothing."
> James 1:2-4

How we respond to those trials depends on several factors. Below are five principles to help you minister to a prodigal's parents.

Principle One

Don't spend your energy trying to get a prodigal's parent to give up hope on their child even when you see them destroying themselves because of the situation.

Help the parents learn the difference between "letting go" and giving up hope. This will include helping them to release their prodigal completely to God and learning to set healthy and consistent boundaries. (See the handout, "Four Steps to Start the Process of Learning to Let Go" at the end of this chapter.)

Each situation carries its own set of circumstances. However, some similarities are clear.

One of the most familiar stories in the Bible is the parable of the lost son (Luke 15). Jesus told this story to a mixed crowd of tax collectors, sinners, Pharisees, and scribes. He prefaced this parable with two others, about lost sheep and a lost coin. Read these stories.

All the tax collectors and sinners were approaching to listen to Him. And the Pharisees and scribes were complaining, "This man welcomes sinners and eats with them!" (Luke 15:2).

Parable of the Lost Sheep (Luke 15:3-7)

> So He told them this parable: "What man among you, who has 100 sheep and loses one of them, does not leave the 99 in the open field and go after the lost one until he finds it? When he has found it, he joyfully puts it on his shoulders, and coming home, he calls his friends and neighbors together, saying to them, 'Rejoice with me, because I have found my lost sheep!' I

tell you, in the same way, there will be more joy in heaven over one sinner who repents than over 99 righteous people who don't need repentance."

The Parable of the Lost Coin (Luke 15:8-10)

Or what woman who has 10 silver coins, if she loses one coin, does not light a lamp, sweep the house, and search carefully until she finds it? When she finds it, she calls her women friends and neighbors together, saying, "Rejoice with me, because I have found the silver coin I lost!" I tell you, in the same way, there is joy in the presence of God's angels over one sinner who repents.

The Parable of the Lost Son (Luke 15:11-31)

He also said: "A man had two sons. The younger of them said to his father, 'Father, give me the share of the estate I have coming to me.' So he distributed the assets to them. Not many days later, the younger son gathered together all he had and traveled to a distant country, where he squandered his estate in foolish living. After he had spent everything, a severe famine struck that country, and he had nothing. Then he went to work for one of the citizens of that country, who sent him into his fields to feed pigs. He longed to eat his fill from the carob pods the pigs were eating, but no one would give him any. When he came to his senses, he said, 'How many of my father's hired hands have more than enough food, and here I am dying of hunger! I'll get up, go to my father, and say to him, Father, I have sinned against heaven and in your sight. I'm no longer worthy to be called your son. Make me like one of your hired hands.' So he got up and went to his father. But while the son was still a long way off, his father saw him and was filled with compassion. He ran, threw his arms around his neck, and kissed him. The son said to him, 'Father, I have sinned against heaven and in your sight. I'm no longer worthy to be called your son.'

"But the father told his slaves, 'Quick! Bring out the best robe and put it on him; put a ring on his finger and sandals on his feet. Then bring the fattened calf and slaughter it, and let's celebrate with a feast, because this son of mine was dead and is alive again; he was lost and is found!' So they began to celebrate.

"Now his older son was in the field; as he came near the house, he heard music and dancing. So he summoned one of the servants and asked what these things meant. 'Your brother is here,' he told him, 'and your father has slaughtered the fattened calf because he has him back safe and sound.'

"Then he became angry and didn't want to go in. So his father came out and pleaded with him. But he replied to his father, 'Look, I have been slaving many years for you, and I have never disobeyed your orders, yet you never gave me a young goat so I could celebrate with my friends. But when this son of yours came, who has devoured your assets with prostitutes, you slaughtered the fattened calf for him.'

"'Son,' he said to him, 'you are always with me, and everything I have is yours. But we had to celebrate and rejoice, because this brother of yours was dead and is alive again; he was lost and is found.'"
Luke 15:1-31

In the story of the prodigal son we read that "While the son was still a long way off, his father saw him and was filled with compassion. He ran, threw his arms around his neck, and kissed him."

"While he was still a long way off." The father expected that his son would return someday. He was a long way off, but the father still recognized him. Why? The father had played and re-played memories in his mind since his son's departure. He knew his son's stride, his build, and his movement. He had never given up hope that his son would return.

Whether or not the parents verbalize it, hope is in their hearts. Often by the time these parents seek help, they have given physically, mentally, emotionally, spiritually, and financially anything they thought would bring their child home. Many times the marriage and remaining siblings have been torn apart by the efforts to win back this one child.

At this point, well-meaning people might encourage parents to hold on to the family they have left and give up their prodigal child. Remember, these parents never give up hope! As a minister, encourage them to learn to let go so they are not destroyed in that hope.

Letting go means helping the parents turn over their child to the Lord fully and completely. Encourage them to let God have control of the situation and not to replay any "what if's" in their minds.

Proverbs 3:5-6 says, "Trust in the LORD with all your heart, and do not rely on your own understanding; think about Him in all your ways, and he will guide you on the right paths."

Letting go also means establishing healthy and consistent boundaries. These healthy boundaries are important whether the prodigal is still living at home or is away. Boundaries also need to be set for when the child might return home, no matter the age.

In Luke 15:17-19, the son finally recognized his own condition and the consequences it had brought into his life.

> "When he came to his senses, he said, 'How many of my father's hired hands have more than enough food, and here I am dying of hunger! I'll get up, go to my father, and say to him, Father, I have sinned against heaven and in your sight. I'm no longer worthy to be called your son. Make me like one of your hired hands.'"

What we see in this son is genuine brokenness. "The son said to him, 'Father, I have sinned against heaven and in your sight. I'm no longer worthy to be called your son'" (Luke 15:21).

Notice that while the father threw his arms around his son and kissed him the father did not call for the robe, ring, or shoes until after hearing his son's brokenness.

Only when parents have learned to let go and turn over their children to God will they be in a position to recognize true brokenness.

Listen to the heart of a mother of a prodigal child.

"One thing I had to learn was to let go. This is the hardest lesson a parent probably ever has to learn. A minister on the staff I was serving with had some difficult issues with all three of his children during their teen years. I asked him one day how he dealt with it and continued to minister to others. He lifted his open hand, palm up, and told me he had to release them to his heavenly Father. I began doing the same thing, sometimes several times a day, trusting God to take care of my daughter and love her more than her father and I did. I continued doing it until I felt the peace of letting go. The alternative would be to go crazy with pain and fear. It didn't eliminate the pain, but it gave me peace in the midst of it.

"We chose to rescue her many times over the years, but there came a point we had to decide whether rescuing was enabling her to continue the path she was on, or helping her. That was a difficult decision to make since things in this kind of a situation never are very clear. Our prayer in not enabling has been that she would come to the point of having to make some changes for her own survival and well-being without anyone coming to her rescue each time she made wrong choices. One of the things we learned was to set some sensible boundaries of what we would be willing to do and on whose terms. A counselor friend said when and if our daughter makes contact, just to listen and not ask a lot of questions. If she is wanting help, even if we did not know whether she was dealing with reality or fiction, we should decide ahead of time what we would be willing to do. Family counseling would be essential if she really did want help.

"We pray for her daily, knowing God is huge and can do anything. I pray for her to find peace with God, restore relationships with others, find help mentally and emotionally, and find true joy. I realize she has a free will and makes her own decisions, but I continue to pray she will listen to the Holy Spirit. I will not give up hope, but I live in peace."

Principle Two

The parents of the prodigal need to be able to assess their responsibility in the relationship issues between themselves and the prodigal. Help the parents to identify areas they may have been able to handle differently.

Matthew 6:14 tells us, "For if you forgive people their wrongdoing, your heavenly Father will forgive you as well." Help them to work through to find forgiveness in each situation.

Colossians 3:21 tells us not to exasperate—irritate or annoy—our children, "so they won't become discouraged." Help them to identify anyone, including themselves, whom they have unforgiveness toward and seek to find forgiveness.

Once the parent understands the principle of letting go, you will want to help the parent assess their thinking and feelings regarding the prodigal child. Many times you will find the parents will blame themselves, the spouse, the child, a sibling (especially if in a blended family), his or her peers, others, God, or any combinations of these for the prodigal's behaviors. Parents will also harbor anger, frustration, embarrassment, fear, helplessness, guilt, or unforgiveness. Identifying these hidden thoughts and feelings is important in preparing the parent's heart to be able to let go and trust God.

Helping the parents work through any emotions of anger, fear, and bitterness toward others is also important. Parents need to be encouraged to understand that imperfect parenting is not the cause for their prodigal's behavior. God is the perfect parent and yet the behavior of His children—past and present—is less than perfect.

If the child has left home, the parents will go through a normal grieving process much the same as a death except without the closure. It is almost like mourning a death over and over again.

Help the parents understand that as parents we all have done some things right and some things wrong. The important thing is to take them through this process so they can get freedom and be in a position to receive the child back.

Listen to the heart of a mother of a prodigal child.

"As a parent of a prodigal, the range of emotions experienced is very wide. Guilt is the first major issue. We tend to blame ourselves for what we did or did not do that might have changed the situation. My husband and I had to come to terms with the fact that we were not perfect parents, but we did all we knew to do at the time to help our daughter be a confident young woman and to turn her life around when she began to stray. It was another part of letting go that we had to deal with to keep our sanity. It's easy to become very angry at the repeated betrayal of a prodigal. Without help, that anger can become dangerous, both to the parent and to the child. Anger is normal and only through God's strength can we be angry and not sin (Ephesians 4:26).

Principle Three

Take time to check on the marriage relationship. A prodigal child situation will always affect a marriage. (If the woman you're helping is divorced or has never been married, skip to counseling principle four.)

Talk with both parents, if possible. Ask them to list on paper how they feel dealing with the prodigal has helped and added difficulty to their marriage. (See the handout, "Marriage Assessment List" at the end of this chapter.) Share with them that honesty is very important to be able to resolve issues that may not have been addressed before.

Because both parents are eager to reach this child, they often take on different approaches as a response to the other parent. For example, if a mother feels a father disciplines too harshly, she will not discipline enough to compensate.

This behavior inevitably builds tension between the parents. Often it's unidentified and unspoken. On the other hand, some parents will do everything by the book and collectively take on the role of failure, which eventually affects their marriage.

Listen to the heart of a mother of a prodigal child.

"During the hardest time of struggle, there was very little physical or emotional strength left to invest in each other. We had a strong marriage, for which I am very grateful. I am not sure weak marriages can survive this kind of crisis. We did try to get away occasionally, just the two of us, but our thoughts would continue to go back to what our daughter was or was not doing. During a period of time when she lived outside our home in high school, we felt a release of some of the 24-hour-a-day stress of wondering what she was doing. Sometimes we even experienced guilt from feeling some relief. But it gave us some time to focus on our other daughter and each other. We prayed together and trusted God to continue to work in and through our situation. When one of us was really struggling, the other was strong. We didn't often fall apart at the same time. That was God's grace! We didn't always agree on how to handle each circumstance, but we desperately needed each other's strength. Our love and commitment held us together when our life was falling apart."

Principle Four

Once the effects the prodigal has had on the marriage have been addressed, help the parents look at the family system as a whole. As you continue to look at the effect the prodigal child has had on the family system, encourage the parents to take time to sit down with each sibling and get a perspective on how they are feeling about the situation.

Regardless of age, some children do not always know how to communicate their thoughts and feelings. This is true especially when a prodigal is involved. The siblings have already observed the effects of the prodigal on the parents mentally, emotionally, physically, and spiritually.

Opening up the lines of communication between the family system is very important. Remember the order of things. The parents need to work through many of their bigger issues before sitting down to walk their children through the process. However, it is also good for the children to see their parents work through some of their thoughts and feelings as well as to allow the children the opportunity to learn how to resolve issues.

Listen to the heart of a mother of a prodigal child.

"Our other daughter was angry at times because of the tense situation in our home. Sometimes she felt neglected. She also worried about her sister and was also angry at her much of the time. We prayed with her and prayed together for her sister. She saw the pain we experienced. She also saw how much we had to invest in her sister during this time, sometimes having little energy left to deal with anything else. As an adult with children of her own, she cannot understand how we have been able to continue in the situation, yet have peace, hope, and joy in our lives. I pray she never has to know."

Principle Five

Supporting the parents and the family so they can continue to move forward with the Lord while the prodigal remains on their reckless course.

Network the parents and family with others who have been through a similar situation. Find other parents who have been able to let go, admit the part they played regarding the prodigal's attitude or behaviors, and reconciled any marriage and family issues as a result of the prodigal's attitude or behaviors. These parents don't have to be perfect, but they're on the road to healing.

Listen to the heart of a mother of a prodigal child.

"The one thing that helped me more than any other thing (other than God's presence, of course) was a friend who had a very similar situation and was transparent with me while my children were still preschoolers. I saw her walk in faith and peace even though she was hurting deeply. She trusted her daughter to God and never wavered in her faith. She was Jesus 'with skin on' for me. When our situation became evident, she was the first person I called because I knew she would understand. If she'd never shared her situation with me years before, I would not have known her openness to help me. I could call and ask her how she got through each day and she would give me words of encouragement and empathy. I desperately needed a mom who had been there. Now I am that mom who shares with other prodigal's parents in pain. I understand the camaraderie in common pain and desire to use my experience to help others walk in faith.

"Counseling was also a huge help, not necessarily for our daughter, but it was for us as her parents. We needed wise advice from an objective source. We were given steps to try to help ourselves and our prodigal daughter."

Resources

LifeWay counseling:
www.lifewaycounseling.org

American Association of Christian Counselors:
www.aacc.net

Focus on the Family:
www.family.org

Boundaries by Dr. Henry Cloud and Dr. John Townsend (Zondervan Publishing House)

Prodigals and Those Who Love Them by Ruth Bell Graham (Baker Books)

Recovering from Losses in Life by Dr. Norman Wright (Revell)

Praying God's Will For My Daughter by Lee Roberts (Thomas Nelson)

Parenting Prodigals: Six Principles for Bringing Your Son or Daughter Back to God by Phil Waldrep (Thomas Nelson)

Use the next few pages as tools to help those who've come to you deal with specific issues. As with all assessment tests in this book, you have permission to print them.

Prodigal Checklist

The following checklist gives some characteristics of a prodigal child.

- hard, rebellious heart toward God and authority

- disrespectful toward others

- unteachable: can't tell them anything, knows all, or doesn't care to know

- attitude of self-sufficiency: doesn't need anyone

- uses those around them for their own means

- see others as blame for their circumstances; cannot or will not grasp a cause-and-effect principle.

- manipulative

- shows no genuine brokenness when confronted with behaviors

- ignores boundaries and not good at setting boundaries for their own life

- wants immediate gratification

- runaway behavior, comes and goes as pleases or has left and not returned

- no regard for how their behaviors affect or interfere with others

- shows no emotions

- says whatever they think the parent wants to hear

Four Steps to Start the Process of Learning to Let Go

1. Admit your state of helplessness.

> "Come to Me, all of you who are weary and burdened, and I will give you rest."
> Matthew 11:28

My paraphrase of Matthew 11:28 is "Bring me your stuff, I'll give you rest."

Notice Jesus says, "Come to Me with the stuff." He doesn't ask us to share with Him what we think should be done, how to fix it, or how to justify or not justify any of it. He just asks us to bring Him our stuff. That is our part. In exchange, He will give us rest.

2. Choose to hand over your child spiritually, mentally, and emotionally to the Lord. That comes with recognizing the truths of God's Word.

> "The LORD of Hosts has sworn: As I have planned, so it will be;
> as I have purposed it, so it will happen."
> Isaiah 14:24

> "'I know the plans I have for you'—this is the Lord's
> declaration—'plans for your welfare, not for disaster, to give
> you a future and a hope. You will call to Me and come and
> pray to Me, and I will listen to you.'"
> Jeremiah 29:11-12

You must remind yourself day by day, hour by hour, minute by minute, and second by second that God is on His throne. He knows all, He sees all, He is present everywhere, and He is powerful enough to do anything. The prodigal is not out of His sight anymore than you as a parent are out of His sight. He is working in each person's life.

3. Stay in God's written Word. Pray it and speak it over all situations and circumstances you encounter.

> Finally, be strengthened by the Lord and by His vast strength.
> Put on the full armor of God so that you can stand against the
> tactics of the Devil. For our battle is not against flesh and blood,
> but against the rulers, against the authorities, against the world
> powers of this darkness, against the spiritual forces of evil in the
> heavens. This is why you must take up the full armor of God, so
> that you may be able to resist in the evil day, and having prepared
> everything, to take your stand. Stand, therefore, with truth like
> a belt around your waist, righteousness like armor on your chest,

your feet sandaled with readiness for the gospel of peace. In every situation take the shield of faith, and with it you will be able to extinguish the flaming arrows of the evil one. Take the helmet of salvation, and the sword of the Spirit, which is God's word. With every prayer and request, pray at all times in the Spirit, and stay alert in this, with all perseverance and intercession for all the saints.
Ephesians 6:10-18

4. Don't journey alone. God intended for us to come alongside one another.

Carry one another's burdens; in this way you will fulfill the law of Christ.
   Galatians 6:2

As a leader, this is your time to help bear the burden of the woman who has come to you for help, support, and encouragement. Encourage others who've been through a similar situation to support her also.

Encourage each other daily, while it is still called today, so that none of you is hardened by sin's deception.
   Hebrews 3:13

Parent's Assessment

1. List the things you recognize that you could have handled differently in the relationship. Confess those to the Lord. Accept His forgiveness. Forgive yourself.

2. List the things you consider that your prodigal didn't handle well in the relationship. Admit those feelings toward your prodigal child to God. Ask Him to help you forgive your prodigal child.

3. List those individuals you felt contributed to the breakdown in your relationship. Admit those feelings to God. Ask Him to help you forgive. Try to discuss your feelings with those individuals.

Marriage Assessment List

Examine the areas that have that have been affected by the situation with a prodigal child. Have both the husband and the wife list these areas.

List areas in your marriage that have become stronger.
(Example: communication)

Husband   Wife

List areas in your marriage that have become weaker.
(Example: financial issues)

Husband   Wife

What issues would you like to discuss with your spouse?

About the Authors

VICKIE ARRUDA resides in Morrilton, Arkansas, where her biblical counseling ministry and Pure Joy International office are located. In June 2008 she resigned her position as biblical counselor on staff at FBC Morrilton, Arkansas, to go full time with Pure Joy International. She has served on staff as a biblical counselor at Great Hills Baptist Church in Austin, Texas, and Gracemont Baptist Church in Tulsa, Oklahoma.

She received her bachelor of science from the University of Arkansas Tech in 1977. After teaching middle school for two years, she returned to school to obtain her master of science degree in school psychology from the University of Central Arkansas.

Vickie traveled with the Great Hills Retreat Ministry, also known as Regeneration Retreat Ministry, for ten years. She has served as chaplain to FCA youth camps and her speaking engagements have included many different conferences related to marriage, parenting, singles, and women.

CHRIS ADAMS is senior lead women's ministry specialist at LifeWay Christian Resources, Nashville, Tennessee. Prior to her employment at LifeWay in December 1994, Chris was the special ministries coordinator at Green Acres Baptist Church in Tyler, Texas, coordinating women's ministry and missions education. She is an ongoing guest teacher at New Orleans Baptist Theological Seminary's Women's Certificate Program, where she received her undergraduate degree in Christian ministry from the seminary's Leavell College. Chris has been a consultant, speaker, and conference leader in a variety of church and denominational roles. She is a contributor and guest editor of *Journey*, and compiled *Women Reaching Women: Beginning and Building a Growing Women's Ministry, Transformed Lives: Taking Women's Ministry to the Next Level*, and *Women Reaching Women in Crisis*. In 2008, Chris received the Career of Excellence award at LifeWay. She is a wife, mother of twin daughters, and grandmother of seven. She also loves reading, good coffee, and chocolate. Visit her blog at *http://lifeway.com/womenreachingwomen*.

6

SEXUAL ADDICTION

Marnie C. Ferree

This chapter focuses on a very difficult issue: sexual addiction. In it you will find specific elements and characteristics about this unique form of addiction. While most of the chapter focuses on the woman who's come to you for help as the sex addict, help also is given for those whose husbands are the addict. As a reminder, your purpose is to inform, support, encourage, and refer the woman who has placed her trust in you as a leader.

One of the toughest topics Christian helpers face is sexual addiction. Even the name is difficult. It immediately surfaces images and connotations most Christians would rather not entertain: a sleazy problem that occurs in smoky clubs that proper people avoid; rooms rented by the hour or during stolen moments romanticized by prime-time television dramas; the soft clicks of a computer mouse in the middle of the night. Sexual addiction is base, is distasteful … is sin.

Pervasive stereotypes surround sexual addiction. Like with any stereotype, they develop because it widely describes a certain issue. Many of these assumptions are true. These pigeon hole descriptions, however, overlook many important characterizations about sex addiction, which the Christian helper must understand if she is to be useful to those who struggle with this shameful problem.

Indeed, shame is the most persistent element of sexual addiction. It is a secret sin that has been around since biblical times, yet it has been denied, ignored, undiagnosed, and untreated for centuries. Those within religious communities have been quick to condemn such sin, and rightfully so. But they also have been unwilling or unable to understand the sexual sinner and offer her the help she so desperately needs.

The shame associated with sexual mistakes is profound. Sexual sin has typically been considered somehow worse than other kinds of sins. When you think of King David, the sin of adultery usually comes to mind before his sin of murder. The fear of being discovered in sexual sin makes it especially difficult for strugglers to ask for help. And when the problem has escalated beyond just a rare or occasional slip into the realm of sexual addiction, the shame can be paralyzing.

Ignorance and misunderstanding about the concept of an addiction to sex is widespread. Knowledge and research is fairly new. Only in the last 20 years has attention been directed toward this area. The whole field is probably at the point where alcoholism was 30 or 40 years ago. Then, people viewed alcoholism as simply moral failure. Most shamed the alcoholic and told her to "just stop!" Today, though, we understand much more about alcoholism, including the proven biological components. Now if someone were to admit to being a recovering alcoholic, she would likely be afforded unqualified respect. Even within the church, the sober alcoholic would probably receive affirmation for facing the problem and turning her life around. Friends would join her in celebrating her recovery.

But when someone admits to being a sexual addict, the reaction is quite different: "You're a what?!" The response is usually horror and disgust. Or fear. Some sex addicts report people avoided them and kept their children away too.

"My friends didn't want me around their daughters," one male addict said. "I've never considered being sexual with a child, but they immediately assumed I was some kind of pedophile."

One female addict's church asked her to leave when she revealed she had struggled years before with sexual sin. She reported, "I felt like I had leprosy."

As if the shame of being addicted to sex isn't bad enough, the stigma of being a woman who struggles with this problem is particularly intense. Our culture has the attitude that "boys will be boys" or that illicit sexual behavior is "just a male thing." A female who has a sexual addiction is considered especially perverted. And a female sex addict who calls herself a Christian? Most helpers simply never consider the possibility. It's too far removed from our notion of women as the standard bearers of morality. The ones who are supposed to keep lustful males in check.

For a Christian woman to admit she's struggling with sexual addiction takes enormous courage. She must first face herself, which is perhaps the most difficult step, then she must risk rejection by confessing her secret. The Christian helper who is the recipient of her disclosure should recognize this sacred trust. It is evidence of both the confessor's desperation and the esteem she has for her confidant. Above all else, this hurting sister needs to be received with the grace and compassion of Christ. Remind her that "all have sinned and fall short of the glory of God" (Romans 3:23) and that "neither death nor life, nor angels nor rulers, nor things present, nor things to come, nor powers, nor height, nor depth, nor any other created thing will have the power to separate [her] from the love of God that is in Christ Jesus our Lord!" (Romans 8:38-39). Before you can begin to help with her behavior, you must help her with her shame. Be gentle with her fragile spirit.

For every woman who dares to ask for help with sexual addiction, many others suffer alone and in hiding. Seventy percent of women keep their cyber activities secret. Definitive statistics are difficult to gather, but according to *http://internet-filter-review.toptenreviews.com/internet-pornography-statistics-pg6.html*, one in three visitors to pornographic websites is a woman. Seventeen percent struggle with pornography addiction—so much so that 13 percent of women admit to accessing pornography at work. Also, women, far more than men, are likely to act out their behaviors in real life, such as having multiple partners, casual sex, or affairs.

In fall 2012, a number of colleagues and I also published a treatment manual for clinicians who work with female sex and love addicts, and part of that process was a small survey of women. We used SurveyMonkey to post a "Women's Sexuality Survey," and out of 491 responses, 261 women identified themselves as sex or love addicts. That number is skewed because we encouraged clinicians working in the field to ask their clients to participate, but it does validate the prevailing view that women continue to struggle with sexual addiction, especially online pornography and other forms of acting out, in increasing numbers.

Despite their surprising numbers, very few women seek help for sexual addiction. Only about 20 percent of those who seek help are women. By offering compassionate, knowledgeable aid, Christian helpers can encourage other women to come out of the shadows and begin a journey toward healing.

Definition of Addiction

Exactly what does it mean to be addicted to sex? First, there's no question that all who engage in illicit sexual activities, including viewing pornography, commit sin in the eyes of God. The biblical standards of sexual purity are clear, no matter how much our sexually saturated society ignores those principles. Sexual activity outside of marriage is contrary to God's plan. And adultery is more than having intercourse with a partner other than one's spouse. The one-flesh union between husband and wife is more exclusive than just physical acts between human beings. Sexual fidelity includes purity of heart, which is automatically violated by using pornography, connecting through Internet relationships, and engaging in all other forms of sexual lust.

When does a woman cross the line from engaging in sexual sin to being addicted? This question is like asking, "How many drinks does it take to be an alcoholic?" No distinct point marks the line between sin and addiction. For most people, that progression can only be clearly seen in hindsight. However, some clear characteristics define an addiction.

Most people who specialize in treating addiction ascribe to the disease model of understanding the process. Don't be sidetracked by arguments over whether addiction is a disease or sin. Of course it is sinful behavior, but it is behavior that follows the course of a disease process. Viewing the addictive process through the lens of the disease model helps us to understand and treat the problem.

A classic definition of an addiction is to have a pathological relationship with a mood-altering substance or behavior. Pathological means diseased—something that's unhealthy. The concept of relationship is important, because addictive behavior is more than just rare or occasional. It's an ongoing relationship with something unhealthy. This pattern of behavior is a key distinction between "mere" sexual sin and sexual addiction. Addiction is an ongoing pattern, not an isolated event. Then the final part of the definition is "mood altering," which means that the substance or behavior is used as a way of purposely altering how you feel.

This disease paradigm helps us understand four key elements of addiction:

1. Compulsive
An addict keeps doing what she doesn't want to do, despite her best efforts to stop. The apostle Paul describes this condition: "I do not understand what I am doing, because I do not practice what I want to do, but I do what I hate" (Romans 7:15). Compulsivity is a hallmark characteristic of addiction.

2. Obsessive

An addict constantly has sex on her mind. Sexual activity—whether doing it, hiding it, or feeling shame about it—is the organizing factor of the addict's life. Everything else is a lower priority. The addiction becomes the addict's god.

3. Continues despite negative consequences

Someone who is addicted doesn't "learn" from her mistakes, but instead, she keeps doing things that clearly get her into trouble. This describes the woman who has been confronted by her boss for pornographic Internet sites found on her computer, yet she doesn't stop surfing the Web inappropriately at work. This behavior is often the one most perplexing to an addict's loved ones, especially in the early stages after they become aware of a problem. At first, people may rationalize that the addict made a mistake during a weak moment. When she repeatedly makes the same "mistake," others wonder why she doesn't "get it" and stop doing ridiculous things.

4. Tolerance

This concept is widely understood when it comes to substances, but many people don't understand that behaviors can create neurochemical tolerance, as well. For the sexually addicted woman, like for all addicts, acting out her behavior is never enough. She'll always want more, either of the same activity or of escalating activities. She'll need more and more to feel the "high" she seeks.

To call sexual addiction a sickness does not in any way relieve an individual of personal responsibility for her sin. This disease model is not an excuse or loophole that gets the addict off the hook. She must still confess her sin, repent, and turn away from her illicit behavior. Viewing addiction as a sickness, however, does explain the complicated nature of the problem. The factors outlined above are why an addicted woman can't "just stop" her sinful behavior. Like treating any other serious disease, the addict must use multi-faceted means to address her problem. In addition to dealing with her spiritual issues, the person must also seek help for the physical, mental, and emotional aspects of her addiction.

Christian helpers need to understand the disease model of addiction to avoid simplistic answers to complex questions. A key mistake is to encourage an addict to tackle her problem simply through religious practices. When you insist that a woman pray more or take part in a Bible study or do something similar as the solution to her behavior, you actually increase her shame. Female addicts who are Christian have almost always already done these things—usually repeatedly—before they finally ask someone for help. If these tactics alone would help, the woman would already have stopped acting out. Addressing the problem through only religious solutions only is incomplete.

Prayer, Bible study, church attendance, and repentance are key to Christian growth. These powerful acts of faith and commitment are key in a Christian's life and key to sobriety and serenity. But these steps alone are not what gets an addict sober. The best way leaders can guide women who are sexually addicted is to encourage them toward complete approaches that have been proven to help. But first, the problem has to be identified accurately. What does sexual addiction look like in women?

Presentations of Sexual Addiction

Often women experience great difficulty in identifying themselves as being sexually addicted. In addition to the denial factor and the shame of accepting that label, there's confusion about the nature of sex addiction. Part of the problem is the belief that this addiction is about sex. In fact, it's not about sex at all.

A Christian woman, married with young children and a teacher in a private Christian school, explains this truth best:

"Why is this called 'sex addiction'? I hate that label! It's not about the sex! Sex is just what I have to give to get what I really want, which is love, and touch, and nurture, and assurance I'm OK."

Some sexually addicted women don't even enjoy the sexual experiences. They either tolerate or endure the sex because of the larger payoff: the connection—however false and temporary—or the medication of emotional pain.

Women also can fail to understand the myriad faces of sexual addiction, which makes it difficult to identify. It's helpful to consider "sex addiction" more of an umbrella term that covers a wide range of behaviors. In a similar way we use "alcoholism" whether the drink of choice is wine, whiskey, or champagne. While there are differences in forms of acting out, they all have the same roots and involve the same dynamics.

Most Christian women shrink from the "sex addict" label and prefer to think of themselves as "love" or "relationship" addicts. It's best not to argue with someone about the label. Simply focus on the presenting problem. The woman asking for help is already ashamed and defensive, and in the long run, the label isn't important.

Self-Test

A helpful tool for pinpointing sexual addiction in women is a simple self test. This isn't a clinical, foolproof instrument, but it's a good starting point. It's adapted from two primary sources: the self test used by the 12-Step group Sexaholics Anonymous and the Women's Sexual Addiction Screening Test, which was developed by Sharon O'Hara and Patrick Carnes.

If a woman has come to you for guidance with a perceived sexual addiction problem, give her this test to take. She can either take it while in the office with you or take it at home. Either place, allow her time to process through the questions honestly.

Women's Self-Test for Sexual/Relationship Addiction

1. Have you ever thought you needed outside help for your sexual behavior or thinking?

2. Have you tried to stop or limit what you felt was wrong in your sexual or relationship behavior?

3. Do you use sex to escape, relieve anxiety, or as a coping mechanism?

4. Do you feel guilt, remorse, or depression afterward?

5. Has your pursuit of either sex or a particular relationship become more compulsive?

6. Does it interfere with relations with your spouse?

7. Do you have to resort to fantasies or memories during sex in order to be aroused or satisfied?

8. Do you keep going from one relationship or lover to another?

9. Do you feel the right person would help you stop lusting, masturbating, or being so promiscuous?

10. Do you have a destructive need—a desperate sexual or emotional need for someone?

11. Does the pursuit of sex or a relationship make you careless for yourself or the welfare of your family or others?

12. Has your effectiveness or concentration decreased as sex or a relationship has become more compulsive?

13. Have you experienced negative consequences as a result of your sexual or relational behavior?

14. Are you depressed?

15. Were you sexually abused as a child or adolescent?

If a woman answers "yes" to even a few of questions 1-13, she is likely sexually addicted. The fact that she's asking for help means she's concerned about her behavior and is willing to at least look at this issue. Remind her that admitting the problem is the first step toward solving it.

Brief descriptions of the main presentations of sex addiction in women are as follows.

Relationship Addict

In general, females' sexual addiction is more relational than males'. Acting out usually involves another person. Certainly, not every woman who is promiscuous is a sex addict, but a pattern of promiscuity or affairs can be a sign of addiction (or potential addiction). This type is repeatedly involved in affairs or multiple relationships, whether she's married or single. These relationships are sometimes serial (happening in rapid sequence, one right after the other), or sometimes they are even simultaneous. Unfortunately, our culture portrays this behavior as normal, especially for a single woman.

Romance Addict

Some women are more interested in the "chase" and intrigue of "falling in love" than they are in the relationship itself. These women are often called romance addicts. They're hooked by the seduction and excitement of pursuing or being pursued. After they realize they've succeeded in snaring their intended, they quickly lose interest. They're unable to sustain a relationship over time. Our mothers' generation called these girls "boy crazy," which is an apt description.

Fantasy Addict

The fantasy addict is very similar. Her relationships, though, exist primarily only in her mind. She can create elaborate fantasies about someone. It doesn't matter if she knows him well, barely, or not at all. The important thing is the fantasy, not reality. She falls in love with the guy next to her at the stoplight or the man she passes in a store. She obsesses about a man she knows and becomes convinced his normal courtesies toward her are a sign of his undying affection. Many Christian women don't recognize themselves as fantasy addicts. They don't masturbate, much less act out with another person, so they never consider they have a problem. But they escape through fantasy and prefer illusion to reality.

Pornography or Cybersex Addict

More and more women are becoming addicted to pornography and cybersex. They're primarily younger women who've grown up in the media-saturated culture. Often they are as reactive to visual stimuli as males typically are.

The main reason for the increase in female pornography addicts is the explosion of the Internet, which has opened a vast new domain for pornography. Key researchers describe the Internet as the crack cocaine of sex addiction because of its "Triple A Engine" of accessibility, affordability, and anonymity. Most women are drawn to the relational aspects of Internet pornography. They get involved in chat rooms and connect with someone online, instead of merely viewing pornography. These women develop intense online relationships, which usually escalate to cybersex or phone sex. Others, however, prefer the visual pornography, whether it depicts opposite-sex or same-sex activity. These women are usually especially embarrassed, because they think their behavior is uncharacteristic for females.

Masturbation

Masturbation is almost always in the picture of sex via the Internet. Self-stimulation is a huge part of cybersex, where the partners aren't physically in the same location. Even without pornography, though, female addicts commonly engage in masturbation. Sometimes this can be a result of molestation they experienced, as they were prematurely introduced to sexual responses. Other times women discover masturbation innocently during childhood as a part of normal, developmentally appropriate self-exploration. In either case, if a woman chooses to masturbate habitually, it can become an addiction when used to alter mood in an unhealthy way.

Exhibitionism

Through the popularization of provocative clothing, today's culture condones female exhibitionism to the point that many women, including Christians, don't give a second thought to showing off their bodies. They simply believe they're being fashionable. Some women, though, exhibit themselves as a part of their sexual addiction. While females rarely expose themselves in the way male "flashers" do, they still can exhibit themselves in ways specifically intended to arouse lust. Much like the romance addict, some of these women become addicted to the rush of being seen and desired.

Addict Who Sells or Trades Sex

Selling or trading sex is another form of sex addiction in females, and this description doesn't just apply to prostitutes. Many female addicts will trade sexual activity for other favors, like expensive gifts or a lavish lifestyle. People often assume that if a male pays for a date, the female rewards him with sexual activity. Because of the dependency of some women, they may feel they have no choice or that they aren't worth a man's attention if they're not sexual with him. A pattern of this "payback" behavior may indicate an addiction.

Stereotypical "Male" Sex Addict

This type of addict most closely conforms to the typecast male patterns of acting out. She has multiple partners independent of any kind of relationship. This woman is sexual with men she doesn't know or just met, like someone she picks up in a bar or some other social setting. Using alcohol or drugs is often part of the picture. This female addict may visit strip clubs or gay bars where sexual activity is rampant.

Cycle of Addiction

Regardless of the form of her acting out, every addict follows a predictable path of behavior. This cycle of addiction was identified by Dr. Patrick Carnes, who is the leading authority on sexual addiction. This cycle sheds light on a key reason women are unable to stop sinful and addictive behavior.

Destructive Consequences

Sex addicts experience a four-stage progression in each addictive episode: pre-occupation, ritual, acting out, and despair. Understanding and breaking this powerful, but predictable, cycle is essential for recovery. Following is a graphic of the cycle of addiction.

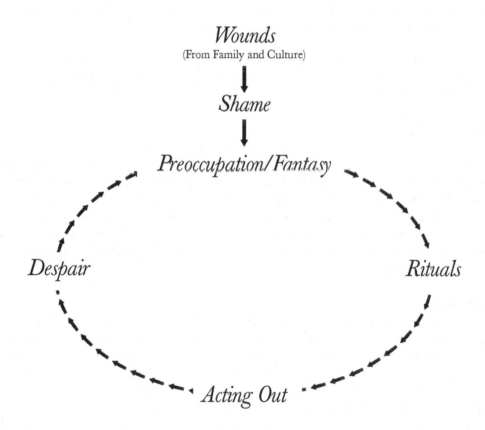

Carnes Cycle of Addiction

At the top of the cycle is wounds and next is shame. A later section discusses addicts' woundedness and the resulting shame, which is the driving force behind the addiction. The focus here is the observable way addicts medicate their internal pain.

Preoccupation

The beginning point is preoccupation, which is also sometimes referred to as fantasy. It's simply the starting place where a woman begins to think about one of two things: either how rotten she feels (emotionally) and/or how she knows she can feel better. The possibilities begin to run through her mind, and she rationalizes what she's considering. Preoccupation is her gateway into the process of changing her mood.

Ritual

Engaging in a variety of rituals moves the addict from the preoccupation/ fantasy stage to the point of acting out. Rituals are as varied as individuals and their own ways of acting out. Some rituals are short, such as a masturbation ritual or one that leads to pornography. Others are longer, such as those that "groom" a potential partner for an affair. They may be blatant or subtle, conscious or unconscious. For many women these rituals of attire, makeup, eye contact, movement, and interaction are so subtle they may be overlooked.

"I thought flirting and being touchy-feely was just part of my personality," Kay observed. "I never realized those kinds of things or going out for coffee with men were part of my rituals."

Acting Out

Through the use of rituals, it's an easy progression to the point of acting out. In this phase of the addiction cycle the woman acts out either with herself, through masturbation, or crosses the "flesh line" to act out with another person. Often, it's only at the point of acting out that a woman realizes she has a problem. She can identify that it's wrong to masturbate to pornography or have an affair, for example. She views the specific behavior(s) as the problem, but she lacks understanding about what led up to the acting out. She thinks she's once again "fallen" into sexual sin.

Despair

Understandably, despair is the last stop in the sexual addiction cycle. Of course the woman feels despair at what she's done. She's acted out again, despite her best intentions. She has broken her promises to herself and to God, and she's overcome with shame. Perhaps she begs God for forgiveness (again) and vows to change her ways. Part of her, however—a deeply secret and hidden part— knows that she won't be successful. Then, as crazy as it sounds, the best way to medicate the pain and shame from acting out is to get lost in yet another round of sexual activity. During the moments of ritual and acting out, the pain can be silenced, or at least, ignored. It's a self-perpetuating cycle.

Consequences

Addictive behavior always exacts a price. Impaired productivity at home or at work, emotional distance in relationships, neglect of responsibilities or children, and certainly shame. For the female sex addict, the price can be much higher. One study found that 80 percent of women who engaged in sexual chat rooms went on to meet in person the partners they had connected with on- line. The associated risk is enormous: dangerous situations, exploitation, sexu- ally transmitted disease. Even if their behavior doesn't escalate into crossing the flesh line, women who spend hours online don't have time or energy for healthy pursuits. Their view of relationships and healthy sexual activity becomes skewed in the heightened (false) environment of the Internet.

What Drives Sexual Addiction

"Sexual addiction" is actually a misnomer, because this problem isn't about sex at all. It's about a longing for acceptance, affirmation, and self-worth—the desperate search for love and touch and nurture and belonging. Those are descriptions of intimacy. They're legitimate needs, but many women don't know how to meet them in healthy ways. Sex becomes a false solution to valid needs and longings. It's a substitution of sexual behavior for the authentic connection of genuine intimacy. Sexual addiction is actually an intimacy disorder, an impairment of a woman's ability to connect with herself, much less with another person in a healthy way.

So what happened that created this breach of intimacy? Why do so few women—indeed, people in general—not know how to be truly "present" with themselves and with others? The answer is complex, but understanding it is crucial if a leader is to be helpful to a woman struggling with sexual addiction.

Family Dynamics

The roots of sex addiction are found in certain unhealthy family dynamics and in our sex-saturated culture. Exploring an addict's family history is not about blame. The objective is to achieve understanding, not to blame or bash someone's parents. Though insight alone isn't necessarily enough to prompt a change in behavior, it's more difficult to make lasting changes without understanding why we do what we do and where our faulty thinking originated. Changing our thinking and our belief system, which obviously is rooted in what we learned in our families, lends fuel to our resolve to change our actions. A change in thinking will also help spawn a change in our feelings.

Families fall somewhere along the continuum of nearly perfect to truly awful. Most parents do the best job they can. They, too, are products of their own families, where they may not have learned the tools for intimacy. In varying ways and degrees, most families are flawed in certain key ways that contribute to unhealthy coping strategies, including addiction.

Rules

A first area is a problem with family rules. These are standards of behavior and relating that are understood, but rarely spoken. Four key rules characterize many families: (1) don't talk, (2) don't feel, (3) deny or minimize, and (4) blame. This environment doesn't allow for healthy communication, where it's acceptable to talk about tough topics, or to feel any of a wide range of emotions. Family members learn to "stuff" their feelings and avoid potentially uncomfortable subjects. Instead of acknowledging problems and dealing with them head on, the family denies that anything is wrong or, at least, that it's very bad. People blame someone or something else for problems rather than accepting personal responsibility. A young woman doesn't learn how to handle life's difficult situations and gets used to deadening her feelings in this kind of environment. It's easy to ignore problems or dodge responsibility by blaming someone else.

Roles

Some families also set up certain roles for members to play. Examples include the heroine, the clown, the doer, the peacemaker, the scapegoat, or the lost child. People get locked into playing one or more roles where they're expected to take care of things or distract the family from its problems or stay out of the way. These roles add predictability and stability to family relations, as well as provide a foundational system that supports the family rules. They also become a mask that a woman learns to wear, which keeps her from knowing her real self. When people are only allowed to act or relate in a certain way, they're unprepared when those tactics don't work in other circumstances.

Boundaries

A third main problem in many families is boundary issues. Sometimes boundaries are too rigid, which means conflict isn't allowed, nor is independent thinking. Family members aren't nurtured in healthy ways. The opposite problem is boundaries that are too loose, which describes an environment where there's little guidance or even abuse. When a woman grows up with boundary problems, she doesn't learn to create healthy boundaries of her own, which leaves her vulnerable to those who might trample over her, or leaves her starved for nurture and affection. Either way, she's at risk to take part in unhealthy sexual behavior.

Other Problems

Many families also suffer from other problems, like some form of addiction, mental illness, violence, divorce, or other issues that drain energy from healthy family functioning. Love often feels conditional, based on performance instead of relationship. When combined, all these dynamics prevent the kind of connection, nurture, and safety that God intended to exist in families. Children don't learn to deal directly with issues, to be in touch with their feelings, or to ask for help. Instead, they learn to navigate life with a boatload of coping skills—like emotional distance, rage, performing, being dependent, drinking too much, working too much, or acting out sexually.

Culture's Contribution

Unfortunately today's society only makes matters worse. Americans value achievement at any cost, wealth, status, and beauty. Values, commitment, honesty, and integrity often take second place. Quite obviously, society esteems sex as a very important commodity. Sex is used to sell everything from cars to deodorant, and personal attractiveness is used as a measure of someone's worth. For example, females compare their bodies to magazine cover girls and see themselves as inferior. Or they learn to flaunt their sexuality to manipulate or otherwise get what they want. Popular media represent sex as another form of recreation or as the measure of a relationship. It's easy, then, for women to be deceived into believing that sex equals love.

Trauma from Abuse

The majority of female sex-addicts have also suffered specific instances of abuse. In groundbreaking research conducted in the late 1980s, Patrick Carnes found that astonishing numbers of adult sex addicts were overtly abused in some way. He found that 81 percent of adult sex addicts had been sexually abused, 72 percent had been physically abused, and 97 percent had been emotionally abused. These experiences of abuse are another key way women are "prepared" for later addictive behavior.

Physical abuse teaches a woman the world isn't safe, so she may look for someone to protect her, who does so at the price of a sexual relationship. Emotional abuse cuts into a woman's self-esteem, so she may be willing to do anything for someone's affirmation and "love."

Sexual abuse, particularly, is a huge precursor to long-term problems with sexuality and relationships. Like nothing else, sexual trauma creates confusion about the relationship between sex and love, especially since most perpetrators of sexual abuse are someone known and trusted by the victim. Many have the mistaken conception that being sexually abused means being dragged off the playground by a stranger in a trench coat (always a male) and brutally raped. Sexual abuse involves many more categories than intercourse. A simple definition is that sexual abuse is when a child of any age (that includes adolescents, who are old enough to "know better") is sexually exploited by an adult for that adult's own purpose or gratification. Inappropriate touching or kissing, therefore, also constitutes sexual abuse.

Trauma of Abandonment

While astounding numbers of sexual addicts are the victims of invasion trauma, not every one suffered in that way. But all sex addicts are survivors of abandonment trauma. A full 100 percent of those who struggle with sexual addiction, both male and female, experienced some form of abandonment. In many ways, the effects of abandonment are more profound than the consequences of abuse. The wounds are deeper, more hidden, and more difficult to heal. Abandonment is the greatest hindrance to intimacy. Some parents lack the skills to nurture a child emotionally. Mom or Dad (or both) may be emotionally unavailable, even though they're physically at hand. Beth Moore refers to a parent's failure to nurture as "a hand withheld," which is a powerful and apt description.

After experiencing neglect in nurturing, it's no wonder a female sex addict seeks out partners who will stroke her and affirm her, including sexually.

Many women today experience sexual abandonment, which is an odd idea in light of our sexually saturated culture. Realistically, though, many females aren't taught specifically about healthy sexuality and relationships. When parents don't impart knowledge and healthy messages about sex, and when the church is silent (other than preaching against sinful expressions of sexuality), children turn to culture—and, perhaps, to pornography—to get their information and satisfy their curiosity. It's just another setup for sexually addictive behavior. Another part of the intimacy disorder that is sexual addiction.

Core Beliefs

A woman's experiences in her family of origin, especially her trauma experiences, program her behavior in influential ways. But trauma also profoundly affects her thinking. Again, without conscious awareness, thought patterns and belief systems are shaped by childhood events. Dr. Patrick Carnes first outlined the four core beliefs of all addicts.

Core Belief 1: "I am a bad, unworthy person."

This sense of personal badness is called shame, which is the belief that "I am someone bad, rather than I have done something bad." Our feelings about our behavior are called guilt. Our negative feelings about ourselves are called shame. Guilt is about performance; shame is about personhood. When a child experiences abuse or abandonment, her only way of making sense of what happened is to blame herself. A child lacks the mental capacity to assign culpability to another person. It's unthinkable for a child to believe her parents may be at fault for her abuse. She's totally dependent on her parents to provide her every need. To imagine that the ones who are supposed to care for her—the ones her very life depends on—may be harming her is simply too scary. The only alternative is that she must be to blame. It must be her fault. Because of her shame, a woman may not believe she deserves to receive healing. She may not pursue it or even let others attempt to help her.

Core Belief 2: "No one would love me as I am."

Trauma creates a shameful sense of being defective. It also spawns the false belief that we are unlovable. *How could anyone love a person who's so fundamentally flawed?* she thinks. The trauma survivor believes that if people really knew her, they wouldn't like her. Worse than that, they would probably leave. As an adult, a woman knows the ways she's coped with the trauma of her childhood. She knows the substances and behaviors she's used to medicate her pain or to find some morsel of affirmation. These activities are her deepest secrets, and she's especially convinced that if others knew this "real" her, they would never love her. Of course, then, she will guard her hidden parts carefully, because she believes it's too dangerous to let the secret out.

Core Belief 3: "No one will meet my needs."

If as a child a woman's most basic needs for time, attention, affection, and nurture aren't met—to say nothing of her physical needs for survival and safety—she fails to develop a sense of the world as a safe place. When our needs are ignored, or worse, we're punished for having them, we come to believe that no one will meet our needs. She concludes that it's up to her to get what she needs, however she can get it. Often those forms of meeting our own needs are far from healthy.

Core Belief 4: "Sex or a relationship is my most important need."
God created us for relationship. He made us relational beings, intended for intimacy with other human beings, as well as with Him. When this legitimate need isn't met (to the extent possible) by our earthly parents, it becomes all consuming. Because of the tragedy of the sexual abuse most addicts have experienced, this God-given need for relationship is often perverted into a need for sex. If the only connected relationship a woman feels is a sexual one, they get merged in her belief system. Or if she must give sex in order to get "love," the same thing happens. It's a trade-off she's willing to make.

Addiction as Coping

Referring back to the graphic, notice that the beginning point of the cycle of addiction is family wounds and next is shame. Addiction is one of the primary ways humans cope with trauma. To recover from inappropriate sexual behavior it's vital to understand and counteract these false beliefs. A woman must literally "be renewed by the transformation of her mind" (Romans 12:2).

Recovery from Sexual Addiction

Jesus offered living water to the woman at the well (John 4:1-26) and grace to the woman caught in adultery (John 8:2-11). Similar hope and healing is available to the sexually addicted woman today. Recovery from sexual addiction is a daily, intentional process that brings freedom from the snare of sexual sin.

The journey begins when a woman answers the question Jesus asked the man lying at the pool of Bethesda: "Do you want to get well?" (John 5:6). For many female addicts, the answer is mixed. A part of her does want to get well. She's in so much pain knows that her life is unmanageable. In Twelve Step recovery language, she's gotten "sick and tired of being sick and tired." But other parts of her hesitates. Does she really want to be "well"? What would it mean to give up her addiction?

The Christian helper nourishes the addict's desire to get well by responding to her with grace and gentleness. Coax out her vision for a different life and remind her to stay focused on that picture. Challenge her to take baby steps and to keep going despite her failures. Instead of scolding her about the effects of her addiction, motivate her with firm reassurance about her value as a child of God. Be her biggest cheerleader.

The First Step: Powerlessness

The journey of recovery begins with an admission of powerlessness over the disease of sexual addiction. Without that acknowledgement, healing will be impossible. Like many other biblical principles, this one involves a great paradox. Salvation comes only through surrender. Only through admitting she is powerless over her sexual addiction can she begin to regain any control of her thoughts and behavior. The White Book of Sexaholics Anonymous (SA), a

12-Step fellowship for sexual addiction, describes it this way: "The crucial change in attitude began when we admitted we were powerless, that our habit had us whipped" (p. 204).

Step One of the Twelve Steps, first formulated by Alcoholics Anonymous, emphasizes this idea: "We admitted we were powerless over alcohol and that our lives had become unmanageable." The Twelve Steps as adapted by the sex addiction fellowships say powerless over "sex" or "lust." As odd as it may sound, there's relief in giving up and admitting defeat in dealing with the addiction on her own.

Like all of recovery, though, this admission of powerlessness is a process, not an event. While there's almost always a single moment when the addict admits her life is unmanageable and out of control, that instance is only the beginning of a true acknowledgement of powerlessness. For most addicts, there's a process of deepening awareness. Allow the woman seeking help to make this discovery in God's timing.

Surrender

After admitting powerlessness, the next steps begin the plan for recovery. Steps Two and Three outline the process of surrender:

Step Two: "Came to believe that a power greater than ourselves could restore us to sanity."

Step Three: "Made a decision to turn our will and our life over to the care of God as we understood God."

Step Two asserts that God is the source of help for overcoming addiction. For many women, even those who consider themselves Christian, taking this step is more difficult than it may seem. Because of their spiritual woundedness, it's difficult for an addict to trust God to meet her needs. A leader can best help by allowing the woman to talk honestly about her negativity toward God. She needs acceptance for her struggles of faith as much as her struggles with addiction.

Step Three calls for an addict to decide to turn her will and life over to God's care and guidance. This decision to surrender is the crucial act. The success of her recovery program hinges on her actions of surrender. It's the point where she "let go and let God." Surrender, though, is also an ongoing process. It's never "done." Innumerable times, in ways both large and small, an addict must admit her powerlessness, acknowledge God's power, and surrender to His will for her life. These first three Steps form the foundation of a journey of healing.

Sobriety

Just as recovering alcoholics talk about becoming sober from alcohol, sexual addicts must abstain from all acting-out behaviors. Sexual sobriety begins when the addict eliminates all sexual activity. That means no masturbation or sexual involvement of any kind, including pornography or cybersex. For the addict whose acting out involves relationship or romance addiction, sobriety would include not being involved in any relationships. A total time-out from sexual and relational involvements is the beginning task of recovery. For the married addict this time-out would obviously include any extra-marital relationships, even those that are "only" emotional affairs. For the single addict that objective would include no casual dating for a period of time.

Community

So how does a woman achieve sobriety, whether she's married or single? The answer is deceptively simple: she heals from her intimacy disorder. The solution for her addictive behavior is to find healthy connection. As simple as that prescription may sound, it's extremely difficult for sex addicts to do. They're intimacy disordered, after all. The very thing that will help addicts heal is one of their greatest fears, because being known risks rejection and abandonment. Almost certainly, a woman coming for help will want to talk with a female leader and no one else. It's vital that a helper insists she invites others into her recovery circle. No one can recover in isolation. No sex addict can heal by herself, or even with the help of a Christian leader or therapist. Some may stop acting out for a time, but it's impossible to recover from an intimacy disorder without practicing intimacy. Being in healthy fellowship with safe people provides the accountability and support all addicts need.

One of the first challenges of recovery is to find emotional safety that allows an addict to risk vulnerability. Ideally, that kind of a safe place exists in the church. Sadly, though, few women are part of that kind of church environment, at least not when the issue is sex addiction. So where can they turn for fellowship?

Twelve Step Fellowship

A Twelve Step "anonymous" group is the best choice. A healthy Twelve Step group is probably the closest model of how the church should function. Members are real with each other. They encourage and hold each other accountable. They invoke God's help and seek His will on a daily basis. They are at places where brokenness meets grace. Some Christian leaders are suspicious of Twelve Step groups and fear they're not biblically sound. Actually, the opposite is true. The first Twelve Step group was founded by Christian men, and their principles come straight from Scripture. One of the best things a helper can do is encourage an addict to become active in a recovery group. It's the best place for her to get practical, long-term help.

A Twelve Step fellowship offers a level playing field, which is comforting for a frightened addict. It's a group of people who all have experienced power-lessness over their sexual behavior and are seeking a different way of life. This common denominator of sexual sin creates an automatic cushion of acceptance. This environment allows the female addict to enter with relative assurance of being understood and accepted. Indeed, most addicts report, "I finally felt like I was home."

Groups for Sex Addiction

Three primary Twelve Step groups exist for sex addiction recovery. The first is Sexaholics Anonymous (SA), which is most closely patterned after Alcoholics Anonymous. This group has the strictest sobriety definition, which prohibits any sexual activity, including masturbation, other than sex with a spouse. SA is more prevalent in the southern U.S. and on the west coast.

The second major fellowship is Sex Addicts Anonymous, which is primarily active in the Midwest. SAA also holds to many of the traditions of AA, but it differs from Sexaholics Anonymous in that members of SAA decide their own sobriety definition.

The third fellowship is Sex and Love Addicts Anonymous, which is targeted at relationship addicts. A benefit of SLAA is that usually a number of women attend the meetings. This group has an inherent flaw, however. Since members in SLAA also determine their own sobriety definition, it's not unusual for a woman in SLAA to consider herself sober because she's only being sexual with one man at a time or only with a man she really "cares about." This definition is obviously outside God's boundary for sexual activity.

As important as it is to connect with a sex addiction recovery group, finding one is often difficult. Though some geographic areas have Twelve Step meet-ings, many others do not. Ideally, you as a leader are aware of the specific groups in your area and can point an addict to help. When there's not a sex addiction Twelve Step group available—or if a woman doesn't feel safe because she may be the only woman there—the best alternative is Alcoholics Anonymous, which is almost universally available. The dynamics are similar for all addictions, and it's absolutely crucial to have ongoing support from other addicts. No matter what group a female sex addict attends, it's important that she practices strict bound-aries. She should take care to connect only with other women and not exchange phone numbers or socialize with male addicts, especially outside of meetings. Often the best group is one for women only, especially early in recovery.

A woman should commit to attend at least six meetings before she decides a Twelve Step group isn't for her. It's an uncomfortable setting at first, and it often takes a while before she realizes how much she benefits from what others share.

The Twelve Steps

Merely attending a Twelve Step support group isn't enough. Lasting recovery requires actually working through the Twelve Steps. Many who are new in recovery fail to grasp what that means. It's an enormous undertaking. It's not enough simply to read the Steps or to think about them or talk about them with a therapist or recovering friend. Actually writing out the lists and inventories is critical. Most women find it takes at least a year to work through the Steps—and that's only the first time. Revisiting the Steps regularly is an ongoing part of recovery. Many excellent resources are available to guide a woman through working the Steps, which follow.

Twelve Steps of Sexaholics Anonymous*

1. We admitted that we were powerless over lust—that our lives had become unmanageable.

2. Came to believe that a Power greater than ourselves could restore us to sanity.

3. Made a decision to turn our will and our lives over to the care of God as we understood Him.

4. Made a searching and fearless moral inventory of ourselves.

5. Admitted to God, to ourselves, and to another human being the exact nature of our wrongs.

6. Were entirely ready to have God remove all these defects of character.

7. Humbly asked Him to remove our shortcomings.

8. Made a list of all persons we had harmed and became willing to make amends to them all.

9. Made direct amends to such people wherever possible, except when to do so would injure them or others.

10. Continued to take personal inventory and when we were wrong promptly admitted it.

11. Sought through prayer and meditation to improve our conscious contact with God as we understood Him, praying only for knowledge of His will for us and the power to carry that out.

12. Having had a spiritual awakening as the result of these Steps, we tried to carry this message to sexaholics, and to practice these principles in all our affairs.

Accountability

For most addicts, the idea of submitting to accountability is less than appealing. Accountability, though, is a key foundation block of a strong recovery. No one can be successful in this journey alone. Without some external factor, it's too easy to give in to the temptation of the moment. It's also important for a woman to have an accountability network, not just an accountability person. Addicts are great at hiding their behavior and manipulating others and can fool just one partner. Being part of a group is vital for long-term recovery. The most effective accountability comes from other addicts, especially from a sponsor in a Twelve Step program, not just from people who care about her. It's also crucial that the woman invites people to hold her accountable, not that others (even Christian leaders) impose accountability on her.

The most effective accountability is practiced daily. It's not enough for a woman to commit to calling her sponsor when she's tempted to act out. At that point, she'll likely to adopt an "I don't care" attitude. Especially in the early stages of recovery, it's critical to call a sponsor every day. Just a brief check-in is fine, as long as it's done every day. An addict should simply report about her sobriety, any temptations or triggers she faces, and how she's feeling.

Boundaries

Boundaries are the protective hedges that safeguard an addict's sobriety. They're benevolent guards that keep her safe. Without boundaries, her best intentions to stay sober will fail. Operating within appropriate boundaries actually provides the freedom to enjoy a different kind of life. Because most women didn't grow up with healthy boundaries, they find it difficult to set them.

The most obvious boundaries are physical ones, and the most obvious example in this category is avoiding sexual activity. That boundary is the bare minimum— just a small starting point. Physical boundaries should include no contact with acting-out partners. Period. No phone or email contact either. A woman whose acting out has involved the Internet needs to establish boundaries around her computer use. It should be in a main room of the house and used only when others are at home. If she lives alone, she may have to disconnect the Internet totally for a while. After deleting problematic sites from her list of favorites, she can install a filtering program that prevents access to pornographic sites and ask her sponsor to review her computer's history file randomly. In general, she should review every aspect of her life. Does she need to change her wardrobe? Drinking habits? Where she goes for entertainment? Who she hangs out with?

Mental and emotional boundaries are also important. A female sex addict must "guard her heart" (Proverbs 4:23), especially if she's in recovery from relationship and romance addictions. Don't entertain thoughts of an affair partner. Stop playing out the "What if?" scenarios. Avoid books or movies that may be triggers. Throw away the mementos and be discriminating about music, which can be extremely powerful.

Counseling

Behavioral sobriety is only the beginning. Unless an addict goes deeper into her recovery, lasting sobriety will elude her and she'll be at high risk for relapse. The journey of recovery, then, is best viewed as a dual track endeavor. One rail is achieving and maintaining sobriety; the parallel rail is healing from family of origin wounds. Resolving the traumas of abuse and abandonment and healing the shame they create are the ultimate tasks of recovery.

Almost always, the recovering addict needs a skilled therapist to heal fully from her trauma. Although a sponsor is invaluable, she rarely is equipped to address deep trauma issues. Most addicts need a counselor clinically trained in trauma resolution and recovery from sexual addiction. Someone without this expertise may do more harm than good.

Again, because of the relative newness of the sex addiction field, locating an informed counselor may be difficult. The best way is to ask other recovering people for recommendations. Ask doctors or mental health professionals for counselors trained in addiction. Contact the local drug and alcohol council for referrals. If a sex addiction specialist isn't available, a counselor familiar with chemical addiction is better than one who doesn't work in this area at all.

For more information on making a referral, refer to the Introduction.

Medication

Sometimes no amount of counseling, trauma work, or any other nonbiological intervention is enough. For some women, medication is necessary. Clinical depression is one condition that usually requires prescription medication. Many cases of post traumatic stress disorder or anxiety attacks also benefit from drug therapy. Instead of numbing the emotions, as some people fear, the right medication can provide the energy and focus to do the hard work of healing. Often it's possible to discontinue the antidepressant or other medication after emotional stability and healing is well under way.

Telling the Story

Possibly the most helpful experience in healing from trauma is simply to tell the story. For a trauma survivor, to be heard and validated is incredibly healing. She must tell the story repeatedly. Because of the enormous shame, one or two times isn't nearly enough. There are a variety of ways for an addict to "tell the story." She can verbally share with safe people, of course. She can write it out in a narrative or assemble a memory book of pictures at different ages and describe the pain of each one. She can create a collage of pictures that illustrate her feelings because of abuse or abandonment. One of the most loving things a leader can do for a female addict is to listen to her story and be with her in her pain. Each repetition releases part of her shame and God's voice of truth becomes louder.

Triggers

It's realistic to assume that the addict will experience ongoing triggers about her addiction history and her trauma history. A trigger is simply a reminder of something in the past, either negative or positive. Some triggers remind her of pain of some sort, whether that's physical, emotional, or spiritual. For example, she sees a TV show or movie about abuse that's similar to her own and she's vividly put in touch with that vulnerable little girl who was hurt. A song may remind her of some romantic time, or a passing whiff of cologne floods her with memories of a particular person. The sight of a scantily clad person or some other sexual trigger activates a rush of brain chemicals and she's overcome with lust. It's impossible to escape or avoid this universal happening. The difference recovery makes is what happens after she's triggered. The benefit of recovery is that a trigger's impact is less, it doesn't last as long, and she's able to handle it without acting out. Her boundaries protect her. Healthy relationships give her safe people with whom to process. Her work around trauma resolution allows her to identify the trigger instead of automatically falling into old ways of coping.

Disclosure

As terrifying as it may be, a married female addict must disclose her acting out behavior to her husband. That's a non-negotiable truth. Healing and true intimacy can never take place in a relationship unless there's complete disclosure. It's simply not possible without the basic foundation of honesty. A deep level of intimacy will never happen if one partner is harboring secrets.

As painful as it is to hear the truth, most spouses long to be dealt with honestly. After all, addicts have consistently lied, and sometimes the husband has felt crazy when she's denied something he knows is true. He deserves to hear the full account at one time, not bit by bit, which prolongs the agony and further erodes trust.

An addict should disclose the general categories of her acting out—for example, whether she's used pornography, or masturbated compulsively, or had affairs, or cybersex, or one-night stands. If others have been part of the activity, she should disclose whether the acting out has been heterosexual or with other women. She needs to tell how much and how long she's been acting out and how much money she's spent. She also must tell any hidden consequences she's suffered that he may not know about.

What the addict shouldn't disclose is the specific details about her acting out. It's not helpful for her husband to know graphic information, like details about sexual positions or response. There's no point in knowing that kind of data, and once it's disclosed, it's almost impossible for a husband to get it out of his head.

An addict's children also need to know some basic information about their mother's addiction. Breaking the cycle of dysfunction in families requires breaking the "no talk" rule. Children certainly don't need any graphic information about the acting out, but they do need an acknowledgement of the problems in the family. A number of helpful resources can guide a woman in age-appropriate disclosure to her children. Check with local therapists for these resources.

Children definitely need to know that a woman is getting help and that it's not their responsibility to take care of her. They should hear that this is an adult problem and that Mom will turn to other adults for help. They especially need reassurance that the problems have nothing to do with them and aren't their fault.

Sharing the Message

John 4 tells an amazing story about the woman at the well who encountered Jesus. She probably was sexually addicted—at least her history of five husbands plus a sixth live—in is good indication. Jesus knew her secret sins, yet He talked with her and even asked for her help. They share a powerful discussion about worship and living water. Then equally surprising, the woman shared the news about her encounter with Jesus. She hurried into the nearby town and told all who would listen about what she had experienced. She was way ahead of any language about recovery, but she naturally was practicing the last of the Twelve Steps: "Having had a spiritual awakening as a result of these Steps, we tried to carry the message to all who still suffer and to practice these principles in all our affairs."

Like the woman at the well, recovering women must spread the amazing message about the gift of redemption from sexual abuse, sin, and addiction. Thousands of addicted females need to hear about the hope of recovery. They need to understand their disease and the process of healing. They need to witness the transformation of women once active in their addiction. The best way for a female addict to maintain her recovery is to give it away.

Spiritual Practices

At its core, sexual addiction is the result of a woman's disordered relationship with God. Her desperate attempts to still her longings through addictive partners or compulsive activity will never satisfy. God alone can fill the aching hole in her soul. Intimacy with Him is the goal of all of recovery.

Step Eleven of the Twelve Steps encourages addicts to maintain "conscious contact with God, asking only for knowledge of God's will and the power to carry that out." Daily prayer is one way to stay connected to God. This isn't just the rote prayer of a woman's earlier days. It's the intentional, real cries of her soul. It's talking with God as she would a friend.

A recovering woman also is wise to have some kind of a daily quiet time. Some people read Scripture, especially from a Bible version that includes recovery material. Others use different books or Bible studies to focus their attention. Many find it meaningful to journal their prayers or gratitude. What's most important isn't what a woman does during her quiet time, but that she intentionally pauses to get present with God.

Practical Issues for Recovering Female Sex Addicts

The steps outlined above are standard for a recovering addict, whether the person is male or female. Unique challenges, however, exist for women who seek to become sexually and relationally sober.

Few Women in Recovery

Female sex addicts, no matter their age or geographic location, share a common belief: "I can't believe I've found another woman who really understands what I'm going through! For years I've thought I was the only one. Nobody talks about this sexual stuff going on with women." Although almost as many women struggle with sexual addiction as men, almost no one talks about it. Finding a supportive community of healthy women is crucial for a female's recovery, but this objective presents some significant challenges. First, most female addicts are resistant to developing relationships with women.

"Women are the enemy!" one female addict declared. "They're the competition. I don't want to relate to other women. I have no idea how to relate to other women."

Practicing intimacy and relationship skills with other women is important for a woman's recovery. Same-sex friendships provide women an opportunity to define themselves as individuals apart from their sexuality or romantic involvements. Finding other women in recovery from sex addiction, though, is often challenging.

Male-Dominated Recovery Groups

Because fewer women seek help, Twelve Step sex addiction groups are predominantly male. It's not unusual for a woman to be the only female in attendance at a recovery meeting. Because of her typical pull toward relation-ships, it's especially difficult for a woman to stay emotionally present and out of her disease at male-dominated meetings. After a period of solid sobriety, at-tending mixed meetings is very helpful, because it helps the female addict see her male counterparts as simply other recovering people who struggle in similar ways. In the early stages of recovery, though, a non-professionally led mixed meeting may not be a good place for the female addict.

Few Female Sponsors

Finding a female sponsor is as difficult as finding safe meetings. Many women must resort to a long-distance phone or email relationship. Online recovery meetings can help women connect, as can attending recovery conferences. In addition to the ones sponsored by the Twelve Step fellowships, the National Association of Christians in Recovery offers an excellent annual conference. Visit *www.NACRonline.com* for more information.

Literature Is Scarce

Another obstacle to women's recovery from sexual addiction is the absence of clinical and self-help literature concerning women's addiction. Most examples in the articles and books are about males' experience. Women need to read about how this disease pertains to them—in information that uses feminine pronouns. A key resource for female sex addicts is *No Stones: Women Redeemed From Sexual Shame* by Marnie C. Ferree. This clinically sound book is the first Christian book written by a woman personally in recovery from sexual addiction. Marnie also directs Bethesda Workshops, which offers specific help (short-term intensive workshops) for female addicts. Visit *www.BethesdaWorkshops.org* for more information.

How Churches Can Respond to Female Sex Addicts

A hugely important task for churches is to be a safe place for hurting people. Churches must refuse to "shoot their wounded," and instead, offer help and hope. In the body of Christ—of all places—women should be free to be real about their wounds and their struggles. Christ's church should be a place where it's acceptable to talk about tough issues.

Jesus rebuked the religious leaders of His day for shunning sinners. He said to the scribes and the Pharisees, "Those who are well don't need a doctor, but the sick do need one. I didn't come to call the righteous, but sinners" (Mark 2:17). The Great Physician clearly understood that those who are sick need a place of healing. A safe church is a place of grace, where sinners are pointed to a Savior who loves them and longs for their transformation.

Churches can help women battling sexual addiction by providing specific resources. The church can serve as a clearinghouse of information about books, counselors, treatment programs, and recovering people who can be helpful to the female addict. The church can sponsor seminars that educate about healthy families and healthy sexuality, as well as about the problems of abuse and addiction. The church can certainly open its doors to Twelve Step or other recovery groups that address sexual addiction.

Hope for Women

No matter how painful her past and how sinful her behavior, it is possible for the sexually addicted woman to "walk in newness of life." Through surrender, she can achieve sobriety. With the tools of recovery, she can maintain integrity.

By the power of the Great Physician, she can heal from trauma. By accepting responsibility and walking in faithfulness, she can re-earn trust. In honesty and vulnerability, she can build intimate relationships. Through grace, she can even come to see meaning in her suffering and sin, as she embraces opportunities to reach out to those women who are still struggling.

Women Married to Sexual Addicts

Female addicts aren't the only women affected by sexual addiction. Realistically, Christian leaders are probably more likely to be approached by women whose husbands are sex addicts rather than by women personally struggling with the issue. These women, too, face shattered lives and dreams. They reel from the shock of disclosure or discovery of their spouses' behavior. They wonder who they can confide in. They're torn between disbelief and despair. *How could this happen to my Christian husband?* they think. Women married to sex addicts also need the help and hope of leaders who understand their pain. She also needs the truth—about her husband's behavior and (surprisingly) about her own.

Three "C's" for Wives of Sex Addicts

Beginning with alcoholism, partners of addicts came together to help each other navigate the difficult road of dealing with an addicted loved one. Eventually, these groups and clinicians recognized three truths regarding the experience of a co-addict. These principles are known as the "Three C's," and they're extremely important for wives of sexually addicted men. They're also probably difficult for her to believe.

Each one is in the form of a first-person statement.

"I didn't cause it."

The most common reaction after a wife's shattering discovery of her husband's sexual addiction is self-blame.
  • What did I do wrong?
  • Why am I not enough for my husband?
  • I know I've gained weight. Am I just not attractive anymore?
  • I admit I wasn't that interested in sex after working all day and dealing with the kids. Is that why he went outside our marriage for sex?

The sexually addicted husband may reinforce these fears. He's probably quick to point out his wife's flaws and may even overtly blame her for his behavior. "If you'd have sex more often I wouldn't have to look elsewhere," he accuses. In her shattered self-esteem, the wife is more vulnerable to believing this lie.

Sadly, the church sometimes echoes the addict's blame. In one congregation, when it became known the minister was involved in Internet pornography, some of the women in the church gave his wife some provocative lingerie. The implication was that if she were more sexual with their pastor, he wouldn't stray.

"I was humiliated and angry," this wife said, "but deep inside, I also worried maybe they were right."

She could be the most beautiful, alluring woman in the world, and still her husband would have fallen into sexual sin. As any addict in recovery will admit, no one is "enough" to curb addictive sexual behavior.

"I can't control it."

The second truth important for a sex addict's wife is the realization, "I can't control my husband's addiction." This mind-set probably runs counter to her immediate response. She naturally wants to control her husband's addiction, and she can think of a hundred ways to try. First, she may punish him by being hateful or curtailing his spending or threatening to throw his clothes into the backyard. Or maybe she takes the opposite approach and thinks that if she rewards him, especially by being more sexual with him, he'll not be as tempted to act out. Maybe she tries to take better care of herself or the house, hoping that will please him. In an endless number of ways she may try to manipulate him to "straighten up and fly right." The truth is that a sex addict's wife is totally powerless to control her husband's behavior. In fact, most of her attempts only make matters worse instead of better and ensnare the wife in her own forms of unhealthy behavior. She is powerless over her husband's sexual addiction. This admission is the first step of the Twelve Steps of a co-addict: "We admitted we were powerless over someone else's sexual addiction and that our lives had become unmanageable."

"I can't cure it."

A similar principle is the admission, "I can't cure it," which takes powerlessness one step further. It's easier to admit a lack of control than to admit an inability to solve the problem, especially one as serious as sexual addiction. "OK, I get that it's not my fault and that I can't control him, but surely I can fix him," is a typically spouse's cry. This desire is legitimate, but again, her approach is usually wrong. Often a wife's "cure" is something like encouraging her husband to move or get a different job. Maybe she buys him self-help books and lectures him about the information they contain. The reality is that none of these approaches deals with the deeper issues that underlie the sexually inappropriate behavior. They're like putting bandages on a gushing wound.

Healthy Choices for Wives of Sex Addicts

So, what can a wife do when she discovers her husband is sexually addicted? How does she respond in a healthy way? The answer is one that's difficult for wives to accept—and critical for Christian leaders to understand. A failure to grasp the following points is the mistake made most frequently by well-intended helpers. The consequences, though, are extremely serious.

Returning to the wisdom of alcoholism treatment, professionals initially thought the alcoholic was the only one in need of recovery. At first glance, it seems logical. After all, what the addict does is so awful, he surely is the "sick" one. Experience, however, showed that spouses of alcoholics also need healing for their own issues and behavior. Addiction is truly a family disease.

The spouse of a sex addict has her own issues. Again, think of an alcoholic family. Frequently, the alcoholic's spouse either enables the drinking by making excuses for the behavior, or else the spouse ignores the problem, even to the point of denying anything is wrong. A similar dynamic is present in sexual addiction.

Like all of us, addicts' wives have learned to cope in a variety of ways, and many of these are quite unhealthy. Almost all co-addicts grapple with codependency. While this is a very broad term which is often over-used, some typical characteristics of codependency exist.

Most of those who are codependent struggle with unhealthy relationships and live unbalanced lives. They have difficulty identifying feelings. They tend to lose themselves in relationships and usually put others' welfare before their own. Codependents suffer from low self-esteem and believe they never quite measure up. Their self-worth comes from the validation of others. They compromise their own values and integrity to avoid conflict or rejection. They attempt to influence and control others' thoughts, feelings, and actions. Codependents, like addicts themselves, believe sex or a relationship is equal to love. They often will use sex to gain approval or acceptance or to keep a relationship.

In essence, codependents are as unhealthy as addicts, they just appear quite different. The truth is that addicts and co-addicts are two sides of the same diseased coin.

Co-Addictive Behavior

Spouses of sex addicts engage in a variety of behaviors that comprise their own version of "acting out," though it's socially and religiously acceptable. These behaviors are mood-altering, just as an addict's behaviors alter her mood. They ease the wife's anxiety or emotional pain, at least temporarily. These actions also are attempts to change or control the addict, but they fail to get the desired result. Instead, they only serve to add depth to the addictive system in the relationship.

One of the most common behaviors is "search and seizure." The wife looks for evidence of her husband's acting out-in his wallet, car, clothing, office, phone records, anywhere. She monitors or spies on him. Based on the information discovered, the wife reacts. Some explode in anger. They accuse and blame and threaten. Others act out by becoming hyper-sexual in an attempt to entice the addicts to stay at home. Still other wives become emotionally distant and shut down, preferring to ignore their husbands' behavior. Another group engages in their own addictions, either chemical or behavioral.

The behaviors may be different, but the result is the same: no healthy changes happen in the relationship.

Wives' Own Woundedness

Often a sex addict's wife has her own experiences of abandonment or abuse. Maybe she carries secrets about childhood sexual abuse or other trauma. One of the saddest aspects of addiction is its power to affect generation after generation. Many addicts' wives grew up with a parent who struggled with some kind of an addiction, so this unhealthy environment feels unconsciously familiar. "My dad was an alcoholic, and I promised myself I'd never marry a man like him," many wives say. "And I didn't—I married a man who was a sex addict and workaholic, instead." That experience is all too common. It's crucial that a co-addict gains self-understanding about how her experiences have shaped her choices, including her selection of a marriage partner. She needs to break the patterns of dysfunction that likely run in her family.

Wives' Own Recovery

The reality of a spouse's own issues emphasizes the importance of her taking own recovery journey, whether or not the addict is willing to get well. Without working on her own issues, a wife is at high risk to enter a relationship with another addict if she divorces her addicted husband. It's another example of the multi-generational pattern of addiction, only this time applied to the codependency side of the diseased coin. Women who doubt that prediction might benefit from exploring their own relationship history. In all likelihood, their romantic partners had some kind of significant problem. Trading one addicted partner for another is certainly no improvement.

Even if the marriage remains intact, the coupleship will never be truly intimate unless both spouses take their own journeys. It takes two healthy people to create a healthy relationship. If the wife doesn't get help for her codependency, which is her own version of an intimacy disorder, the marriage won't be the wonderful union God intended.

Encouragement for the Christian Leader

To be a Christian leader of believing women is an awesome responsibility and a wonderful blessing. Those called to this undertaking have a duty to offer informed counsel to those seeking help. A leader's commission is to be Christ's hands in giving comfort and his voice in providing direction. A leader's blessing is to see the Healer at work in hearts and lives where there once was no hope. And in the process, to deeper her own walk with the Comforter and Counselor.

Resources

No Stones: Women Redeemed From Sexual Shame, Marnie C. Feree (ISBN: 1-591600-16-2) available through the Bethesda Workshops ministry online at *www.BethesdaWorkshops.org* or call toll-free 866-464-HEAL.

National Association of Christians in Recovery (NACR): *www.NACRonline.com*

Bethesda Workshops: *www.BethesdaWorkshops.org*

Sexaholics Anonymous (SA): *www.sa.org*

Sex Addicts Anonymous (SAA): *www.sexaa.org*

Sex and Love Addicts Anonymous (SLAA): *www.slaafws.org*

Codependents of Sex Addicts (COSA): *www.cosa-recovery.org*

Overcomers Outreach, Christian group for any addiction: *www.overcomersoutreach.org*

Alcoholics Anonymous (AA): *www.alcoholics-anonymous.org*

About the Author

MARNIE C. FERREE, M.A., is the founder and director of Bethesda Workshops, a Christian-based clinical intensive workshop for sexual addiction recovery. The program she established in 1997 for female sex addicts was the first of its kind in the country. Marnie is a licensed marriage and family therapist and a certified sexual addiction therapist.

Her book, *No Stones: Women Redeemed from Sexual Addiction*, is unique in addressing sexual addiction in women. She is the editor of *Making Advances—A Comprehensive Guide for Treating Female Sex and Love Addicts* and serves on the editorial board of the *Sexual Addiction and Compulsivity Journal*.

NOTES

7

INFERTILITY

Kaye Hurta and Chris Adams

Even if you personally have not experienced infertility, a large number of women in your church and throughout your community are struggling with this issue. As leaders we must be prepared to provide spiritual and practical help.

Some women may eventually become pregnant, some may adopt, and others may never have children in their home. No matter the situation, we need to come alongside these hurting women and be the hands and feet of Christ.

My sweet friend Chrissie had just been told by her doctor that she would be unable to have biological children. Following her infertility diagnosis, Chrissie came to see me. My conversation with her started with a simple question, "How are you feeling about it and what are your thoughts around it?"

Her eyes welled up with tears and what poured out were thoughts and emotions that were deep and painful and not resolved with simple answers.

As I listened to Chrissie share her heartbreak, I felt a familiar pang of sadness and loss in my own heart. My husband and I were married 15 years before we adopted our first girl. Nearly 12 years and two daughters later, I feel my own eyes well up as I revisit the feeling that somehow I disappointed my husband and failed to give him a biological child—a "mini-him." I believe wholeheartedly that there is not an ounce of regret for him, but still my heart feels the ache.

Like most life losses, experiencing infertility is not something you "get over" or "solve." Instead, you learn to live with the wound and lean into the healing and satisfaction that only the Spirit of God can provide.

For a seemingly straightforward issue, infertility is wrought with complexities. For Chrissie, her strong emotions about her infertility were umbilically tied to childhood trauma and the shame associated with that.

Chrissie's situation is unique to her, but the underlying emotions are consistent with what I have heard from many women. They are discouraged, disheartened, and hoping against hope they might be able to have a child.

Chrissie reported that she felt like a failure … and guilty that she couldn't do this for her husband and her family. She felt like God was punishing her in some way or that He just didn't want her DNA passed on.

How she was thinking says something about what she felt, and how she felt drove her behavior. *What did I do wrong?* and *Now what is my purpose in life?* were questions that haunted her. These are common questions and painful thoughts.

With diagnosed cases of infertility on the rise, chances are you already know someone who is struggling with this problem. It is vitally important to have a map to help her navigate her pain.

Understanding the Issue

Fertile. Just saying the word conjures up images of a lush, green, well-watered, productive landscape. What images come to mind when you hear the word "infertile"? Infertility is a major life event. The inability to conceive can profoundly affect how a woman feels about herself, her husband, her friends, and, of course, God.

According to the Centers for Disease Control and Prevention, 6.7 million women between the ages of 15 to 44 are infertile—approximately 11 percent of the female population in the United States alone.[1]

While a woman may feel the shame and sole responsibility of being unable to have a biological child, it is by no means strictly an issue about women. Studies show that 40-50 percent of infertility cases involve factors related to the male.[2]

Medically speaking, "the inability to conceive after a year of unprotected intercourse and the inability to carry a pregnancy into its full term characterize infertility."[3]

There are three different classifications of infertility: primary, secondary, and situational.

A woman with primary infertility is unable to conceive and bear a child.

Secondary infertility is the inability to conceive or bear a child after having successfully had a child. This is uniquely devastating to the woman as it takes her by surprise; she just does not see it coming.

Situational infertility refers to the woman who needs medical assistance in order to reproduce. Her situation is unique because she perhaps desires to be a single parent, is of advanced maternal age, or is identifying with the GLBT community. (While this may be a rare case in your ministry experience, it is on the rise in our current culture and we need to be prepared. More on this in the "Helping the Hurting" section)

Additionally, there are four stages of trying to conceive:
1. Trying to conceive naturally
2. Diagnosis of infertility
3. Infertility treatment
4. Resolution of infertility

"Each stage carries its own level of stress … Studies have found that men and women dealing with infertility can experience chronic stress on the same level as patients dealing with deadly diseases."[4]

Infertility takes a heavy toll in nearly every area of a woman's life. It affects friendships, family relationships, finances, her spiritual foundation, and even her recreational pursuits. However, the most profound effect will be on her marital relationship.

A woman struggling with infertility is experiencing a wide range of emotions, such as sadness, loneliness, fear, anger, disappointment, loss of control, shame, blame, jealousy, guilt, anxiety, and isolation.

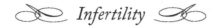

The most profound emotions she deals with are loss and depression.

Loss. From the moment a little girl holds her first baby doll, she begins dreaming of the day when she will marry and have a baby of her own. For a woman facing infertility, this dream has died. In her heart, she is grieving a death. She grieves the death of the dream of giving birth, breast-feeding, passing on her family genetic heritage, and so much more. She may be cycling the emotional stages of grief—denial, anger, and bargaining, depression, and acceptance. Grief is not linear; you do not start at one point and neatly cycle through until it's over. It is more like a Slinky, with twists and turns, good days and bad. Grief is best worked out in community, not in isolation. Staying isolated in your grief can easily lead to depression.

Depression. A study by Alice Domar, PhD, "has clearly documented that women who've been diagnosed as infertile are twice as likely to be depressed as a control group, and that this depression peaks about two years after they start trying to get pregnant. And even though infertility is not life-threatening, infertile women have depression scores that are indistinguishable from those of women with cancer, heart disease, or HIV."[5] If the woman you are helping is seriously depressed, please make a referral to a counselor, psychiatrist, or medical doctor. (See also chapter 4 on depression.)

Understanding the basics of the issue of infertility is straightforward. Understanding how to effectively care for the heart of a hurting woman is a bit more complex, but well worth the effort.

Helping the Hurting

In my experience with helping those who are hurting, it has been useful to have mental hooks to help organize my thoughts. The framework that works best for me is *personal preparation;* the *ministry of presence;* and *referrals, resources, and pastoral care.* Nearly everything you need to minister to a woman in crisis will hang on one of these hooks.

Personal Preparation

Your own physical, emotional, and spiritual health is paramount to being an effective helper. Care for your own soul; stay connected to your own small group and church; share life authentically and vulnerably with others; and grow in your intimacy with the Lord, your personal prayer life, and knowledge of His Word. Understand your own wounds and wrestle down your painful issues with a trusted friend, mentor, or counselor. Please do not make your ministry time about your own pain or try to meet your own needs through helping—this only hurts you both.

The Ministry of Presence

In this life, pain is inescapable. The abundant life was never intended to be a pain-free life. Instead, the promise from Scripture is the promise of His presence, His person, His peace, His redemption, and so much more. Pain significantly affects us at the heart level, and it is a primary pathway to spiritual maturity. Pain will shape us whether we choose to engage or disengage with it. Disengaging is avoidance and requires us to numb our pain in some way, which can lead to destructive behaviors or habits. Engaging our pain and stewarding it well grows our character and deepens our relationship with God and with others. A spiritually healthy view of pain is the desired outcome when we minister to women in pain.

If God gives you the opportunity to stand with someone in her pain, consider this sacred space. It bears repeating: if God gives you the opportunity (the privilege) to stand with someone in her pain, consider this sacred space. It is your invitation from the Spirit to communicate the heart of Jesus—quite often, without words. This is what I call the ministry of presence.

The ministry of presence includes the following activities:
active listening
showing empathy
praying

A woman facing infertility is a woman in crisis. What does a woman in crisis need beyond the ministry of presence? Not much. Here are some general guidelines for an effective ministry of presence.

Active Listening. Her story matters, so listen to her story. A simple starting question—"How can I help you?"—or invitation—"Tell me what's on your heart"—should get the ball rolling. While she is sharing, please listen, really listen. This is not the time to coach, teach, fix, solve, or share. Just listen to her.

Listening often involves silence. Don't be afraid of silent space; the Spirit of God may be using it to speak to her and to you. Wait in the silence.

Listening involves looking. As she is sharing, look at her—not your watch, your iPhone, your calendar, or your shoes. It's too probable that the one time you look away will be the one time she looks at you and senses you've lost interest. Then you will have lost her trust. Take note of her expressions and emotions while she is telling her story—is she stoic, sobbing, inconsolable? If she is crying, offer her tissues but resist the urge to hug her. Crying is a good thing, a healing thing. Hugging can be stifling; it can communicate, "There, there. Stop crying." Touch her arm, hand, or knee to express care, but hold off on the embrace.

Listening involves listening—not sharing. She is telling you her story, so please refrain from chiming in with your own story: "I remember when I was your age and I had a miscarriage" or "My daughter is infertile too; I know how you feel." It is dismissive and unkind to make this time about anyone else; it's about her. The best thing to say in the face of loss or grief is "I'm so sorry" or "There are no words." Repeat, if necessary.

That said, her sharing might lead you to ask probing questions, but do so tenderly and gently. She has probably already asked her OB/GYN about medical options, so you do not have to provide them or ask for details. If she offers this information, great. An appropriate question to ask after her story is "How can I help?" She probably knows what she needs. If she does not, that information is hanging on the referrals, resources, and pastoral care hook.

Also important to remember is the devastating effect infertility can have on a couple's marriage. She may come to you with grief over childbearing, but a deeper issue could be the breakdown of her marriage. Men and women communicate differently and grieve differently. It is OK to ask how things are going with her spouse.

Listening involves nonjudgmental loving. Express genuine care and concern for her. Love her no matter what she is telling you. Earlier I mentioned situational infertility. Suppose she is telling you about her infertility because she has chosen an alternative lifestyle. Please do not register shock, disdain or disapproval. Grieve with her first; earn the right to speak into other areas of her life as the Lord gives the opportunity and at another time. Love her first and then let there be some time and prayer before you address other issues.

Showing Empathy. There is a big difference between sympathy and empathy. Sympathy cares and shares the feelings of another but keeps its distance. Sympathy says, "At least you _____" or tries to find the unseen benefit. Sympathy wants to make things better. Empathy, on the other hand, is an action. It is an action of understanding and experiencing the person's emotions and experience without necessarily having a personal frame of reference. Empathy enters in. Empathy makes a choice to connect and stand with, cry with, walk with, and pray. Be empathetic; connect with her heart first, not her head.

Praying. Praying for people is foundational to our faith. Praying over them or with them builds their faith as well. Pray with her, and as you do, she will learn about the role of faith and hope through prayer. Another way to "pray" for her (or them as a couple) is to write out prayers on note cards for her to read. Often, when we are depressed or our hope is fading, we do not have the energy to pray. Reading written prayers can be a faith lifeline.

159

Referrals, Resources, and Pastoral Care

Referrals and Resources

Unless you are a professional counselor, you will likely refer this woman to someone in the professional community. Create a network of resources and referrals for women in crises of all kinds. The very best we can do for women in our ministry is to link them with the best of both worlds—the support of the professional community along with the love and care of your pastoral response or women's ministry team.

You may already have a counseling referral network in place. If you don't know where to start, consider contacting a large, Bible-believing church in your area for their referral list. Most larger churches have a pastoral care or counseling department to help you build your list. In addition, the American Association of Christians Counselors *(www.aacc.net)* has a link to help you find a Christian counselor in your area. Other online referral resources include *www.find christiancounselor.com* or *www.christiantherapist.com.* The introductory chapter to this book also gives you insight and direction on how and when to make a referral and how to set up a list of referrals and community resources.

Here are some helpful resources for infertility:
Larry Crabb, *Shattered Dreams: God's Unexpected Path to Joy* (Colorado Springs: WaterBrook Press, 2001)
James R. Dobson, *When God Doesn't Make Sense* (Wheaton, IL: Tyndale House, 1993)
Jennifer Saake, *Hannah's Hope: Seeking God's Heart in the Midst of Infertility, Miscarriage and Adoption Loss* (Colorado Springs: NavPress, 2005)
Sittser, Jerry. *A Grace Disguised: How the Soul Grows through Loss.* (Grand Rapids: Zondervan, 1995)
Resolve Organization: *www.resolve.org*

Pastoral Care

If you have permission to share a woman's struggle with infertility with your ministry team, try the following suggestions for care:

• If needed (for example, a death through miscarriage), arrange for meals to be brought to the family.

• Write simple cards or emails that express care.

• If they are comfortable with visits, then visit. No one wants to feel loss *and* isolation.

• Call occasionally to check in, but always ask first, "Is this a good time to talk?"

• Organize a prayer time with the couple if they want, praying with a small team in their home or someone else's.

• Remember and acknowledge difficult days, such as Mother's Day and Father's Day or the anniversary of the loss (if there is a miscarriage).

• If your church offers Grief Support, offer to attend with her, if it helps.

• Organize a small group for people struggling with infertility and allow them to connect and belong.

DO:

Do be an empathetic listener first, not a sharer.

Do encourage her to share her story and give her space and time to do so.

Do remember her husband is grieving and will need support as well.

Do acknowledge her loss, especially if she has had previous miscarriages.

Do pray with her, not just for her.

Do ask permission before you share her situation with anyone else on your team. Confidentiality matters!

Do continue to care and be available, but remember to set personal boundaries.

Do use Scripture, but use it wisely! Hearing her story and knowing where she is spiritually will help guide you in this. However, even the most mature believer does not find comfort in being reminded how happy she should be that she will see her baby in heaven one day. Rejoice with those who rejoice and mourn with those who mourn! Let her grieve first.

DON'T:

Don't ever, ever, ever start a sentence with the words "At least …" "At least you can adopt. At least you have one healthy child. At least you'll see your baby in heaven. At least you have a husband who loves you." Never.

Don't make this about your own pain or past struggles. Never say, "I know how you feel." You don't. You can empathize, but you cannot know.

Don't answer for God. Don't offer *why* answers or promises that God will deliver.

Don't offer cliché spiritual statements like, "God has a plan. He will work it all out for His good in His time." All true, but the Spirit will whisper those truths to her broken heart. In time, He may use you to do it, but the moment of her crisis is not the time.

Don't attempt to solve or fix her infertility. Medical professionals can give her direction here.

Don't tell her what she "needs" to do or "should" do. "You need to be more involved with other women. You should come to _____." It's true that healing happens in community, so invite and offer, but don't prescribe.

Endnotes

1. "Infertility," Centers for Disease Control and Prevention, accessed January 28, 2014, *http://www.cdc.gov/nchs/fastats/fertile.htm.*

2. Gerard M. Honoré, PhD, MD; Jay Nemiro, MD, *Overcoming Infertility: A Woman's Guide to Getting Pregnant* (Omaha, NE: Addicus Books, 2010), 1.

3. "Hidden Secrets of Infertility: Infertility Statistics," accessed January 28, 2014, http://newinfertility.com/infertility-statistics/.

4. William Schoolcraft, MD, HCLD, *If at First You Don't Conceive: A Complete Guide to Infertility from One of the Nation's Leading Clinics,* (New York: Rodale, 2010), 233.

5. Christiane Northrup, MD, *Women's Bodies, Women's Wisdom—Creating Physical and Emotional Health and Healing Revised and Updated* (New York: Bantam Books, 2010), 416.

Chris Adams's Story

I love Kaye's practical suggestions and direction in this chapter. For someone who grew up constantly playing with dolls and babysitting, I thought becoming a mother would be an easy and natural course for me to take after getting married at 19. My career plans including being a wife and a mom, period. So when we had been married a couple of years, we decided it was time to start our family.

I experienced all four stages of trying to conceive and, might I add, some of the stages were extremely difficult. Please be sensitive at certain times of the year—like Mother's and Father's Days—that can be especially hard for infertile couples. Perhaps a focus on spiritual motherhood and fatherhood would be in order on these days.

I had developed some health problems several months before our wedding, but the doctor said then the only difficulty it might cause in trying to get pregnant is that it might take me a little longer because of the endometriosis. So, we were not surprised when a few months went by without becoming pregnant. But after several more went by, we decided to consult a doctor. This began a journey of infertility specialists, tests, surgery, and monthly highs of hopes for pregnancy coupled with lows of finding out it did not occur yet again.

As I watched many of my friends getting pregnant, sometimes for the second or third time, I began to become somewhat bitter and jealous of my friends and even angry with God. All I'd wanted was to get married and raise children. I'd loved children all my life. Why would He not give us a child?

During a special weekend at our church, we were challenged in many ways to allow God to have full control of our lives, including our wants, hopes, and desires. We were instructed to write our burden, or whatever we were holding back from God, on a piece of paper, then to go into the worship center, tear it up, and leave it on the altar. I knew God wanted me to put this issue of pregnancy on the altar. When I did, it was more than just symbolic; I truly was able to give God my heart in this issue. I realized for the first time it was not up to me at all whether I ever had a baby. I was also able to say it was all right either way, and I meant it. I did ask Him to take away the desire eventually if His plan for us did not include children. As long as that desire was there, I believed one day He would answer our prayers for children.

But God's plan for our marriage and our lives was the most important thing for us, not whether we became parents. The bitterness drained out of my heart and left assurance that God was in control. When I left my burden on that altar, a journey of spiritual transformation began that continues to this day.

Wouldn't it be nice to say it was all easy after that? But that wouldn't be completely true. What I can say is that there was inner peace even as I continued to desire a baby. The end of the story is that several more years passed before our prayers were answered through the adoption of twin daughters. Not only did He answer, He did it doubly.

But what if He had not answered this way? What if He had had other plans for us that did not include children? I don't guess I will really know for sure, but I believe that He would have given me the grace to allow Him to reign and to fill the void of being childless with His own presence. I know without a doubt there are incredible things He has taught me through the struggles of infertility—things I do not believe I would have known had I not gone through that experience. Since that time, there have been many other difficulties, and through each one I've learned things about Jesus that I did not know. He does provide peace that makes no sense, and He has proven His faithfulness over and over again. That is why I know He would have led us in victory through childlessness had that been His plan for us. That's the kind of God He is. Not only does He give us His presence and peace, but He grows us through the experience. Then He allows us to use those experiences to minister to others going through the same thing. God has given me the privilege of walking with others on the road of infertility because of my own journey.

My encouragement to you as a leader is to encourage a support group for the women (or couples) who are dealing with infertility. How wonderful to have had one when I was in my twenties and often hurting in isolation since "all my friends were pregnant" or so it seemed. Let those in this support group discuss their experiences, but have a leader who has experienced infertility and has chosen to trust Christ through it all no matter the outcome. That way, she can help these women move from feeling like victims to being victors! Or just connect one infertile couple with another couple who has experienced this situation.

Ultimately, women must decide for themselves if they really believe God is good and has a perfect plan for their lives. We can't force women to this place, but we can certainly model it. Encourage her honesty, commit to pray for and with her, be sensitive with conversation, be willing to listen, provide resources on infertility (see end of chapter) and help her find a place to serve. Be patient as you minister to these precious women and pray for God to move in each heart as you journey with them.

Resources

Dear God, Why Can't I Have a Baby? by Janet Thompson
Infertility by Cindy Lewis Dake
Shepherding Women in Pain by Bev Hislop
Counseling Women by Dr. Tim Clinton and Dr. Diane Langberg
The Infertility Companion by Sandra L. Glahn, ThM, and William Cutrer, MD

About the Authors

KAYE HURTA has a master's in counseling from Liberty University and is a crisis counselor for women's events through LifeWay Christian Resources. She also leads worship for the You Lead events.

Whether speaking, singing, or listening, Kaye's passion is to help others find intimacy with Christ and soul transformation through the living pages of His Word. "I was a wounded, lonely Midwest farm girl until the Divine Romancer swept me off my feet. I want to steward my story well so that others can find Him in their stories and be fully satisfied."

Kaye met and married her husband Chris in Austin, Texas, in 1987. They have two daughters, Madison and Cami, through the miracle of adoption. They live in the Chicago 'burbs where Chris is a pastor at Willow Creek Community Church and Kaye serves on staff in pastoral care and grief support.

CHRIS ADAMS is senior lead women's ministry specialist at LifeWay Christian Resources, Nashville, Tennessee. Prior to her employment at LifeWay in December 1994, Chris was the special ministries coordinator at Green Acres Baptist Church in Tyler, Texas, coordinating women's ministry and missions education. She is an ongoing guest teacher at New Orleans Baptist Theological Seminary's Women's Certificate Program, where she received her undergraduate degree in Christian ministry from the seminary's Leavell College. Chris has been a consultant, speaker, and conference leader in a variety of church and denominational roles. She is a contributor and guest editor of *Journey* and compiled *Women Reaching Women: Beginning and Building a Growing Women's Ministry, Transformed Lives: Taking Women's Ministry to the Next Level,* and *Women Reaching Women in Crisis.* In 2008, Chris received the Career of Excellence award at LifeWay. She is a wife, mother of twin daughters, and grandmother of seven. She also loves reading, good coffee, and chocolate. Visit her blog at *http://lifeway.com/womenreachingwomen.*

NOTES

NOTES

# NOTES

NOTES

NOTES

 NOTES

 NOTES

NOTES

More Valuable Resources for Your Women's Ministry

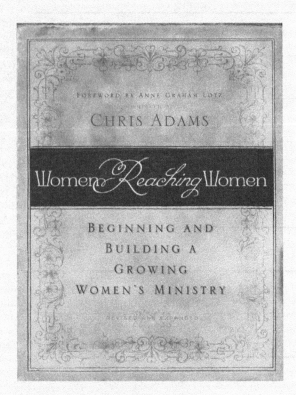

WOMEN REACHING WOMEN:
Beginning and Building a Growing Women's Ministry
Compiled by Chris Adams
This is the one book every women's leader needs on hand for quick reference and biblical guidance. Whether you're beginning or building on a well-established ministry, you'll find this revised and expanded comprehensive guidebook a time-saving and trusted resource.

Paperback 001293365 $16.95

TRANSFORMED LIVES:
Taking Women's Ministry to the Next Level
Compiled by Chris Adams
This revised and expanded edition expands the foundational plan for beginning an effective women's ministry. Move women from being the objects of ministry to serving those around them, learn about spiritual gifts, minister to special needs, and develop strong leaders. Includes how-to budgets, creative childcare, related resources, and more. Each chapter offers suggestions for adapting to the needs of a smaller church.

Paperback 005371579 $16.95

LET'S BE FRIENDS!

VISIT OUR LIFEWAY WOMEN'S BLOG AT
lifeway.com/allaccess

Women's Ministry
Training Pre-conference
with Chris Adams

lifeway.com/youlead

LifeWay Women | events